The Joys of Easter

Books by RACHEL HARTMAN

The Gifts of Christmas

Days of Grass (editor)

The Joys of Easter

by RACHEL HARTMAN

Illustrated by RAGNA TISCHLER

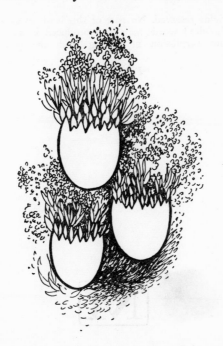

MEREDITH PRESS

New York

Library of Congress Catalog Card Number: 67-11027

MANUFACTURED IN THE UNITED STATES OF AMERICA FOR MEREDITH PRESS

VAN REES PRESS • NEW YORK

To my parents
whose lives have glowed
with the joys of the
Resurrection

Foreword

THERE are joys of Christmas and joys of Easter. Something which begins at Christmas is culminated at Easter. But Easter is also a beginning.

As the gift is symbolic of Christmas—God gave His Son —so joy is the best possible expression of the mood of Easter.

Fear and discouragement are much a part of the human condition, but Easter took the sting out of death, replaced discouragement with hope and fear with love. It is interesting that every time a heavenly visitor appeared, the people to whom he came had to be told not to be afraid. Even when Jesus showed Himself to His disciples after Easter, He had to say "Fear not" to those who perhaps should have understood.

We fear change, thinking it might be for the worse. Sometimes we miss the blessing that change can bring for the better. We fear the future because we have not been there. We fear all that is, and sometimes those who are, different. Sometimes, like the people who lived in Gadara, we accept the subnormal because we fear having things changed to normal. They preferred having Legion—the man possessed by many demons—mad rather than clothed and in his right mind, because it meant change in their lives, too.

But Easter upset everything. Whoever heard of a man who was innocent of any crime—not only of the one for which he was condemned—suffering without complaint and asking that those who killed him be forgiven? Whoever heard of a man's being killed in full view of hundreds of people and later appearing alive with as many eyewitnesses to his aliveness as to his death? Whoever heard of a handful of uninfluential people, many of them uneducated, changing the course of a world?

One of the greatest proofs of the Resurrection is the change that came over a number of fearful, vacillating, ordinary people. The message of Easter is "Fear not. . . . Rejoice and be exceeding glad." Let us contemplate the many joys of Easter.

R.H.

Contents

The Joys of Easter

I. *The Joy of Anticipation*

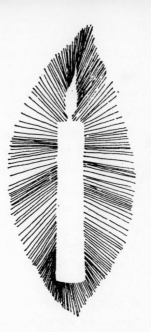

IS the pleasure of anticipation greater than that of realization? It is a question that has been variously answered throughout human experience.

Young people work up extravagant enthusiasm about what they can do—often quite unrealistic thinking. Those who have had success and happiness in life—along with the normal amount of failure and distress—are the ones who can really anticipate.

We tell a discouraged person, "You must have hope" and we are right, because more things are accomplished by hope than this world dreams of. Tennyson said this of prayer, but isn't prayer made up largely of hope? Anticipation of a better life, a better community or world, is what keeps us working at all that is altruistic.

We hope our children will have full, happy lives, so we encourage self-reliance and try to teach them the importance of self-discipline. We want them to reach out joyfully for whatever life will bring them, so we give them satisfactory experience with hope. No parent is able to fill all of a child's wild hopes for material things—nor would it be good preparation for that child's future. But part of the preparation for happy, useful adulthood is learning to anticipate good.

A child in a loving home looks forward to Christmas, remembering what a wonderful time it was the year before. A young mother was startled at the vehemence of her two-year-old's "No!" when told that it was her birthday, and there was going to be a nice celebration. Finally the mother recognized Jenny's problem: The only birthdays she could remember were those of other members of the family. She had begun to get a little tired of someone else being the center of attention. When Jenny finally realized that the presents and the cake were for her, she was all smiles. Another year she may be able to anticipate if she can remember the pleasurable experience.

Anticipation is a powerful thing. It can help you put up with all sorts of inconvenience in the present. It can provide new energy to work harder at accomplishing the desired end. Perhaps it even helps to bring about what is anticipated—whether good or bad.

Anticipating a pleasurable experience—a visit with loved persons, an evening of entertainment, a restful or exciting vacation, an achievement or recognition—this is the stuff that makes life worth living. Those who always hedge themselves against disappointment—"It probably won't work," "He won't really come," "I won't be able to do it"—are not living fully because they aren't trusting themselves to life.

When adults express great delight in anticipation, we call it childlike and often find it quite charming. We have much to learn from children. Usually their hope comes from the fact that they have loving parents. And we all can hope because of a loving Heavenly Father. "Except ye... become as little children, ye shall not enter into the kingdom of heaven."

Lent is a time of anticipation. As the expectancy of Advent is climaxed by the happy feast of Christmas, so Lent with all its serious aspects looks forward to the commemoration of the greatest triumph of all, the Resurrection.

Allied to the joy of anticipation is the joy of being well-prepared. More than any other time of the year, for the Christian, Lent is a time of preparation. Most churches hold special services during this time, and parishioners are urged to accept certain disciplines, though Protestants generally do not observe a fast.

Our English word *Lent* has no religious meaning; it probably comes from the Anglo-Saxon *lengten*. Lengtentide was the time when days were lengthening, springtime. Germans refer to the period as *Fastenzeit*, fasting time. Christians living on the island of Malta have adopted for Lent the Moslem word for fasting, *Ramadan*. For those who wish to keep a time for meditation but not self-denial, Lent is as appropriate as for those who wish to fast.

Originally there was only a two-day fast, from Good Friday to Easter. Actually it was kept for forty hours, commemorating the time Jesus was in the tomb. The devout ate nothing at all during that time. The idea for fasting came from the verse Mark 2:20: "But the days will come, when the bridegroom shall be taken away from them, and then shall they fast in those days." Later the fast was extended to all of Holy Week, then to include the week before. Sundays were always excepted, and in the Eastern churches Saturday was not a fast day, either. During the third and fourth centuries churches gradually adopted the forty-day fast.

One might ask, "Why forty days?" The main reason given is that that was the length of Jesus' temptation in the desert. Some have related it to the Israelites' forty years of wandering in the wilderness before entering the Promised Land. Another suggestion is that Old Testament prophets kept forty-day fasts.

Athanasius, Patriarch of Alexandria, Egypt, commented that in the year A.D. 337 "the whole world" fasted for forty days. However, with Sundays free, people weren't actually fasting for forty days, so in the seventh century, Pope Gregory moved the fast up to begin four days earlier. This made exactly 40 days to fast plus the six Sundays before Easter, making Lent begin on a Wednesday. The ecclesiastical term for Lent, Quadragesima, comes from the forty days.

Food is not the only thing which is limited during the Lenten period. The Roman Catholic Church does not use the word *Alleluia* in song or liturgy during that time. No weddings are performed, in some churches no flowers appear on the altar, purple vestments are worn during Mass, and even the organ is silent from the Gloria of the Mass on Holy Thursday through the Gloria on Holy Saturday. At royal courts Lent was a time of mourning, with the women dressed in black and no ornaments. In rural sections of

Poland not too long ago, dancing and singing were banned during Lent.

Though no weddings are performed during the period, Lent has always been a traditional time for matchmaking in Ireland. In Germany and Austria, Laetare Sunday was a day to announce engagements. In Bohemia that was the proper day to propose, via a go-between.

In early years fasting was rigorous. No meat or by-product such as milk, cheese, butter, or eggs was allowed, and often only one meal a day was eaten. In the ninth century the fast laws became less rigid, but not until the nineteenth century did people generally eat breakfast on fasting days.

Those who did not fast for reasons of health were expected to make contributions to the Church. In France the Cathedral of Rouen has a steeple known as the Butter Tower, built from money given by those who did not fast milk foods. In 1918 the Catholic Church lifted the restrictions on "white meats," the term for milk, cheese, and butter, entirely. The northern countries—Britain, Ireland, Scandinavia—never did have such restrictions. Significant changes in fasting laws announced by Pope Paul in 1966 are related to the Vatican Council and the renewal of the Church.

In most countries Lent begins with Ash Wednesday, which was called simply "Beginning of the Fast" until 1099 when Pope Urban II gave the day its present name. In some parts of Austria and southern Germany, the beginning of Lent was announced at midnight by the solemn ringing of church bells. They rang again on Wednesday morning to call people to the ceremony of ashes.

Ash Wednesday is not observed in Eastern Orthodox

churches because their Lent begins the previous Monday. The day is called Clean Monday, probably because the house is clean of restricted foods by that day.

The custom of putting ashes on the head was at first only for "public sinners," but by the eleventh century it had become universal. Even popes submitted to the imposition of ashes, walking barefoot to the church for the ceremony.

"Public sinners" were persons of prominence, usually, who had committed serious public sin that had caused scandal. If they wished to be received back in the good graces of the Church, they could do penance from Ash Wednesday until Holy Thursday, but the penances were very severe. They wore hair shirts and sackcloth, went barefoot and slept on the ground or on straw. They were forbidden even to stay with their families or enter the church. Often they lived at monasteries doing manual labor or acts of charity and praying. They were not allowed to bathe or cut their hair. In some cases they were even forbidden to speak to other persons. On Holy Thursday the public penitents presented themselves at the church barefoot, unshaved, and in sackcloth. After being absolved, they rushed home happily to bathe, shave, and get ready for Easter.

The custom, which began in the fourth century, is now extinct, but a word remains in our vocabulary as a result of the practice. Since the period of public penance lasted forty days it was called quarantine. The first definition of quarantine in Webster's dictionary is still "a period of forty days," though we usually associate it with the idea of separation, not time.

In England, the four days before Lent begins are referred to as Shrovetide: Egg Saturday, Quinquagesima Sunday,

Collop Monday, and Shrove Tuesday. In olden days Egg Saturday was a time for children to go Lent-crocking, which may have been the origin of our Halloween trick-or-treat custom. The children went from house to house demanding meat or eggs. If they were refused, they threw broken crockery at the door of the house.

Collop Monday was the last day meat could be served, since the fast grew progressively more restrictive. Collops were pieces of dried or salted meat, as steaks were pieces of fresh meat. Even the collops prepared months before must be used up before the beginning of Lent.

Shrove Tuesday has many names—Pancake Day from the traditional food served, Goodish or Goodies' Day because of the good things to eat. In France it was often referred to as Bannock Tuesday, in Germany *Fastnacht*, or Night of the Fast.

Poland called the days before Ash Wednesday Fat Days. In old Russia Butter Week was a holiday before the very strict fast, when even fish was forbidden on some days and all theaters and amusements were closed. It is no wonder people wanted to have a good time before entering the rigors of the nearly seven-week fast.

In our country the festival time before Lent is called Mardi Gras, though actually Mardi Gras means Fat Tuesday and refers to the day before Ash Wednesday. It is a legal holiday in Alabama, Florida, parts of Louisiana, Panama, and the Canal Zone. Probably because of its popularity as a tourist attraction, the festivities in New Orleans have been extended to ten days.

The New Orleans celebration is supposed to date from 1827 when some young Creoles, who had returned from schools in Paris, got together to celebrate as they had done in France. They wore fantastic costumes and danced in the streets of the French quarter. Then, as now, adults followed youth in their styles of entertainment. Where balls were formerly only held indoors, some now moved out into the streets, and the custom remains to this day.

Biloxi, Mississippi, has a Mardi Gras celebration which the citizens claim started earlier than the one in New Orleans. Mobile, Alabama, has had a thriving festival since 1830, and there are accounts of masks and costumes to celebrate carnival from much earlier. Tourists from all over the U.S. converge on these cities for carnival time to watch the leader of the Mystic Krewe of Comus cavort with his subjects. His identity is kept secret, but Rex of Mardi Gras is always a prominent citizen who is honored by the appointment.

Mardi Gras is the climax of a very social period. The

season of carnival begins on Twelfth Night and continues through Shrove Tuesday. The word itself means "farewell to flesh or meat." Carnival was once celebrated all over Europe, and remnants of the festivities remain, notably at Nice, on the French Riviera, and in Munich, Germany. In old Russia they drove a fantastic figure called the Butter Goddess around the streets on a decorated sled. Special folk songs were reserved for the season, and the favorite food was *blinni*, an unsweetened pancake. At the end of the week, the goddess was burned with great festivity. The folk aspects of the spring festival still remain, though without any connection with Lent.

Fire seems to be an important element in Lenten folk customs, as is water. The old practice of the boys' sprinkling the girls with water during carnival time or at Easter —the girls retaliated the next day—goes back to the fertility rites of pagan days. The people reasoned that plants needed water to grow and develop and so perhaps people did, too. The pagan influence is strong in many Lenten traditions.

Brandsonntag or Fire Sunday was the first Sunday in Lent in southern Germany. Wooden wheels or rings with flaming sticks attached were rolled down the hillsides at night. In France that day is called *Fête des Brandons* or the feast of Torches, because young people used to run through the streets with firebrands, apparently to chase away winter. In another old custom a straw figure dressed in white to symbolize snow was burned, drowned, hanged, or buried, depending on the region. Even today the third Monday in April is a festival called *Sechselauten* in Switzerland's largest city, Zurich. Postcards and travel folders

tell the tourist that this is the time when with great ceremony they burn "Boog" or Old Man Winter. Basel, one
of Switzerland's Protestant cities, has a gay carnival complete with masked dances and processions and practical
jokes.

Usually the church and the municipal leaders frowned
on excesses at carnival time. Riots broke out occasionally
in which people were injured or killed. In old Vienna the
carnival masquerades were finally banned from the streets
and allowed only indoors at carnival balls.

In New Orleans, carnival ends with the burying of the
sardine on Ash Wednesday. It isn't really a sardine but a
thin strip of meat which is buried with mock solemnity
to mark the end of Mardi Gras.

In the Greek Church the Lenten fast begins on Monday.
At vespers the evening before, the priests wear red vestments, since that is the color for penance in that part of
the world as is purple in the West. Church illumination is
cut to a minimum and the priest prays with the people the
ancient prayer of St. Ephraem the Syrian:

O Lord and Ruler of Life, take from me the spirit of idleness,
despair, cupidity, and empty talking. But grant to thy servants
the spirit of purity, meekness, patience, and charity. Yes, O
Lord, grant that I may see my own sins and not judge my
brother. For Thou art blessed for ever and ever. Amen.

Then the priests ask each other's pardon. The people do
the same, embracing each other. Each time pardon is asked,
the response given is, "God will forgive you." The idea, of
course, is that they may enter the fasting period with a
clean conscience. It is what gives Shrove Tuesday its name

in the West. *Shrove* is the past tense of the archaic verb *shrive*, meaning to confess one's sins or to impose penance.

The first Friday in Lent is a very special day, known throughout Protestant churches as World Day of Prayer. It is exactly what the name suggests, for all over the world on that day small and large groups, particularly of women and young people, gather to pray for each other and for peace. This observance which started eighty years ago, is kept in 140 countries and territories. Some prayer meetings are held very early in the morning, some during the day, others in the evening, so that united prayer is being raised at some place all during the day. In recent years a planned service has been conducted with the programs printed in the many languages. The United States World Day of Prayer is sponsored by United Church Women, part of the National Council of Churches, though other groups also participate. Monies collected at the services go to support colleges, literacy programs, mother and child care, and many other needy activities abroad. The sharing is world-wide, though. Women of other countries have sent offerings here to relieve distress they had heard about.

Midway through Lent an interesting break occurs in the solemnity of the season. Laetare Sunday (*laetare* is Latin for "rejoice"), which gets its name from the first words of the Mass for that day ("Laetare, Jerusalem" which was considered to be addressed to the Second Jerusalem, the Church) was a time for celebration of ancient spring customs. In some places the burial of winter took place then. In Poland children carried figures of the stork through the village, certain to bring good luck to the town. In parts of Italy and France, Laetare was called Fontana or Sunday of Fountains. It was the day to decorate the town's wells and fountains with flowers and leafy branches. This undoubtedly has pagan origins.

In England, Laetare took on a distinctive character, as Mothering Sunday. At the time of the industrial revolution, young people left the farms to go to the city to work, the young men in factories, the young women as domestics. But this one Sunday they returned to their homes to visit their parents and often to the home church. It became the custom to carry one's mother a simnel cake, made with raisins and currants, which had been blessed by the parish priest. The cake is probably named for a fine flour called, in Latin, *simila*. Early simnel cakes were boiled, then brushed with egg and baked, leaving an extremely hard outer crust. An old saying went, "He who goes a-mothering finds violets in the lane." While the custom of Mothering Sunday, much like our Mother's Day, is not carried out as faithfully as in other days, remnants of the custom remain in the elaborately decorated simnel cake, covered with marzipan frosting, which is a part of the English Eastertime.

The fifth Sunday in Lent is called Passion Sunday, sometimes Silent or Quiet Sunday. In Catholic and Anglican churches, all images are veiled until the first Mass Easter morning. On Friday of Passion Week, in Latin countries, the Feast of Seven Sorrows commemorates the sufferings of Mary. In Central Europe the old custom was to serve a meal with seven bitter herbs: watercress, parsley, chives, nettle, sour clover, primrose or yellow cowslip, and spinach.

While the majority of Protestant churches do not expect their people to fast during Lent, many of them expect parishioners to make certain sacrifices in order to enter more meaningfully into the spirit of the season. For some people Lent is a burden, a time when it is necessary to do without something one likes very much. Yet in our comfortable, well-dressed, gadgeted lives, it seems almost sacrilegious to call doing without candy or cigarettes or theater dates sacrifice. Not many Americans know much about sacrifice. One wonders if fasting has much meaning to such a well-fed people.

Another point of view is that Lent is a time, not for

subtraction but for addition, not an opportunity to take
something out of life, but to add something that will make
a significant difference in the life. Those who hold this
view attend church services more often during Lent or
observe the practice of private devotions more carefully.
Others take on a course of devotional reading. These addi-
tions can make the period particularly meaningful.

Many persons feel they would like to know more about
the Bible, and this is a good time for reading it. Sometimes
a different version brings freshness to the text and renewed
appreciation for the familiar passages. There are many
books to help the lay person understand the Bible better.

Religious writings of former days are excellent reading
during Lent. This is a time when many persons become
acquainted with sacred classics and such writers as Thomas
à Kempis, Brother Lawrence, Lancelot Andrewes, John
Wesley, François Fénelon, Madame Guyon. There is a
great deal of enriching devotional material of a recent date,
including such writings as those of Catherine Marshall,
J. B. Phillips, Pierre Teilhard de Chardin, C. S. Lewis, Paul
Tournier, and Dietrich Bonhoeffer.

If the performance of good habits or enriching activities
adds a new dimension to one's life during Lent, probably
these should be continued throughout the year. Lenten
reading may develop new interests which bring renewal to
a life or a church. Lent does not mean deprivation but
discipline. Instead of subtracting, we should be adding good
things during the period.

Anticipation is heightened as the goal is neared. And as
the weeks of Lent stretch into Passion Week and then Holy
Week, the anticipation reaches its climax. There should be

an element of desire, of wanting, in looking forward to Easter, but some persons dread the gloom and seriousness of the last week. Jesus "set His face to go to Jerusalem" we are told, though He knew what was going to happen to Him there. It was a different sort of anticipation, because He knew the joy that exists in the midst of suffering.

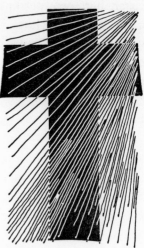

2. *Joy in the Midst of Suffering*

THERE is a great paradox in that title. Suffering, which causes unhappiness, seems the antithesis of all that is joyful. Yet all of us have known the phenomenon of joy in the midst of suffering.

Perhaps it has been a person we have observed who, while in anguish or pain, yet found much to be happy about. Even the homely, "It could have been so much worse. I'm grateful it turned out this way," is a small picture of this. Sometimes we have learned after a long time that a particularly cheerful person has been carrying a terrible burden, which could have crushed another. We think, What courage! But it is more. That person has hidden springs of joy which refresh him in the midst of his suffering.

Some have said that suffering is essential to joy. In the intensity of young love, pain and the sweetness are mixed. And in parenthood the suffering—or perhaps it should be called endurance—is a part of the joy of having children. Those who can shield themselves from hurt with a callous or careless spirit are not those who experience the greatest joy.

Jesus knew where He was going when He started toward Jerusalem. He told His disciples several times that He was headed for crucifixion, but always He coupled this with resurrection. The writer of the Epistle to the Hebrews tells us that "for the joy that was set before him," Jesus "endured the cross, despising the shame."

Holy Week commemorates the most important happenings of history, to those who call themselves Christians. It is a week of mixed emotions. The hurrahs and parade atmosphere of Palm Sunday, the anger and strength of the Cleansing of the Temple, melt into the gentle poignance of the Last Supper, the lonely anguish in the Garden, the injustice of the Trial, the humiliation of the Scourging and Crucifixion, the sadness and emptiness of the Burial.

But those of us who know the whole story—who have experienced this reenactment before—know that the grave is not the end. That ahead is victory, the triumph of Easter, the most hopeful note in all human history.

Holy Week was once a time in which no regular work was done, though it was far from a holiday in our sense of the word. Everyone was expected to attend interminable

religious exercises, amusements and hunting were forbidden, children had to be less noisy than usual. Every year several prisoners were pardoned. One wonders whether this perpetuated Pilate's custom of releasing prisoners during the Feast of Passover or whether these were people who should never have been jailed according to our present standards. In medieval days rulers customarily took retreat in a monastery during the very solemn period.

figures depicting Passion scenes are carried through th[e] streets while great throngs gather to watch.

Balconies and the windows of tall buildings are much in demand as the procession comes by. Some firms rent space for their employees to watch from. The floats, carried on the shoulders of strong men, are owned by *cofradías*, which were once trade guilds and are now family or social groups. Each year the *cofradías* add to the finery the statues wear and march in the procession with the figures. In the city of Málaga there are at least twenty-seven *cofradías*, each with appropriate symbols and distinctive costumes. Each has a name representing an event in the Crucifixion story and parades two groups of sculpture, one showing the scene for which it is named, the other featuring a weeping madonna adorned with jeweled eyes and tears. The carriers are dressed in colorful ancient costumes, and the floats are surrounded by penitents, wearing long robes and pointed, conical hoods which cover their faces except for eye slits. The black or brilliant colors of the robes and hoods identify the groups and present a striking scene.

The anonymity of the hoods in Spain represents penitence rather than stealth, but for many Americans the fifteenth century costumes look too much like the present-day Ku Klux Klan's to be quite comfortable. Bakery shops sell pastries in the shape of the hooded penitents as well as crown-of-thorn cakes. *Semana Santa*, Holy Week, is the climax of the fair which has been going on for weeks. This procession is not conducted by the Church—the ecclesiastical procession honoring the Passion is on Corpus Christi Day in June. The *Semana Santa*, a strange mixture of pagan

Palm Sunday, which commemorates Jesus' procession into Jerusalem, riding a young donkey, while well-wishers and followers shouted encouragement and threw down coats and tree branches in the way, has always seemed a strange break in the solemnity of the Lenten period. Rather triumphal hymns are sung in church that day, children are given palms to carry home, and the atmosphere is one of festivity, while everybody knows that the week it opens is the most solemn of the year.

Some recent writers have proposed that we have been wrong in thinking of the procession as a triumph, that actually it was a great failure. Jesus allowed the people to stage the parade, but it only demonstrated that they had misunderstood Him, that they were looking for a political leader to free them from the army of occupation which was administering the country. They didn't seem to understand when He said, "My kingdom is not of this world" and "The kingdom of God is within you." Perhaps we should keep this as a day of penitence, asking where we have misunderstood God's purposes, where we have been waving palms when we should have been washing feet or otherwise ministering to the needs of others.

Every year on Palm Sunday the Franciscan Fathers from the monastery in Jordan lead a procession from Bethphage, the village where the disciples found the ass and colt tied, to the church of St. Anne in Jerusalem, tracing as nearly as possible the route of Jesus' triumphant ride. They cannot go through the Golden Gate through which He entered the city, because it has been permanently sealed pending "the return of the Lord."

Perhaps the best known of present-day Palm Sunday

ceremonies is the elaborate procession in St. Peter's Basilica in Rome, when the Pope is carried in on the shoulders of his attendants while others carry great branches of palm leaves, some elaborately festooned. The Palm Sunday procession and blessing of the palms originated in the Frankish Kingdom. Earlier, at least in Italy, people went to Mass carrying a twig of olives.

In medieval days palms were blessed at a chapel or shrine outside of town, and the people marched to the cathedral or main church. A wooden statue of Christ on a donkey, the whole thing on wheels, was drawn in the procession. As the procession reached the city gate, a boys' choir would sing. After salutation of the image or the Sacrament—and sometimes this was carried instead of the statue—the people knelt in prayer, then spread carpets and cloths on the ground, throwing branches and flowers in the path of the procession. Church bells pealed and the crowd sang, "Hosanna." Sometimes the procession was limited to the churchyard, where families knelt at the graves of relatives. In France and England it is still customary to visit and decorate graves on Palm Sunday. Palms, a symbol of triumph over adversity, were widely used on the tombs of the martyrs and are in every form of Christian art.

In Greece the day is called Sunday of the Palm-Carrying or Hosanna Sunday, but in areas where palms are unavailable, the day has taken on many names—Branch Sunday, Willow-twig Sunday, and Flowering or Blossom Sunday, depending on the particular substitute for palms. Sometimes it was Fig Sunday, and bunches of figs were given to children in remembrance of the barren fig tree which was cursed by Jesus. Another name was Spanish Sunday, be-

cause children made a drink from Spanish licori water. The English used the term Chare or Sh which comes from the idea of clearing the a Easter.

Of course people could always name some "palm," and still call the day Palm Sunday. In call the yew "palm," because of its use on that d has its palm-willow and Germany its *Palmkätzc* kittens, or what we call pussy willows. Ukr Poles had a ceremony in which they used to other gently with the pussy-willow "palms" or day. The exercise was called *Boze Rany* or God and represented the scourging of Christ.

In Russia palm branches, artificial flowers, ar tied with wax fruits were placed before the fr On the other side of the world, Mexicans cel Sunday by carrying crosses decorated with flo and cakes to church.

In Sicily there was a superstition about Palm the weather. Dust from the floor of the churc tered on the fields. This apparently had some with ensuring a good crop, and, too, the directi blew would indicate the prevailing wind for th A clear Palm Sunday meant good weather, abu and fruit.

Wednesday of Holy Week has been a day in tries for housecleaning. This is probably an ou the Jewish idea of cleaning house before Passov this day begins the elaborate pageantry of Holy which preparation is made all year, when elabor

and Christian elements, has become a folk or civic custom carried on with the full approval of the state.

Maundy Thursday is an interesting name whose origin is somewhat uncertain. Most writers believe that it comes from the Old French *mandé*, from the Latin *mandatum*, meaning "command" or "mandate." These relate to the words of Jesus which are read that day: "A new commandment I give unto you, That ye love one another."

There is also the suggestion that Maundy may come from the Anglo Saxon *maund* or basket, because it was the custom for titled women to go about with a basket on that day, distributing alms. The first Queen Elizabeth is said to have done this. One wonders if the alms basket has anything to do with the origin of the children's Easter basket.

On Maundy Thursday Elizabeth I is also supposed to have washed the feet of a poor person, using a basin of warm water in which were floating sweet-smelling herbs and flowers. Today the Queen gives money to the poor to perpetuate the custom.

Foot washing still has a prominent place in the keeping of the day, however. It is customary for the Pope to wash the feet of thirteen of his officials at St. Peter's in Rome. Twelve of them represent the apostles, but the thirteenth is for the angel who is said to have appeared at the table when Gregory the Great was carrying out the custom in the sixth century. In Spain, where people wear black on this day, the archbishop washes the feet of thirteen aged poor persons at the cathedral. Afterward they are wined and dined with city and religious dignitaries and taken to see the pageants.

The day used to be called Green Thursday. Before the

thirteenth century, priests wore green vestments on this day; public penitents who were being restored wore or carried sprigs of green and were called "green ones." In Central Europe traditional Green Thursday food was green herb soup, spinach with boiled or fried eggs, meat and green salad.

The names "Shere" or "Chare" Thursday, also used for this day, were thought to come from the custom of bathing and shaving or trimming the beard in preparation for Easter, infrequent events at that time. Because of the rigors of cleaning up, fasting was not required. However, it is more likely that the words refer to being purged of sin (*schere*) and to a turning or returning (*char*).

An old legend says that Christ fell into the river Cedron on His way to Gethsemane. So the custom arose in Slavic countries for men in the rural districts to rise at midnight on Great Thursday and walk to a brook to wash.

Most English-speaking people and Latins use the term "Holy Thursday," Ukrainians call it Thursday of the Passion, and the Greek Church refers to it as the Holy and Great Thursday of the Mystic Supper. It has also been referred to as Kiss Thursday because of the kiss of Judas.

In Protestant churches it is increasingly the custom to hold a communion service on Maundy Thursday, commemorating the Last Supper. Some attempts have been made at realistic recreations of the meal which Jesus shared with His disciples. And a number of churches, with advice from Jewish friends, serve a Passover meal and end it with the service of Holy Communion.

In old Europe church bells were silent or hit with wooden clappers from Thursday night until Sunday. The children were told that the bells had "gone to Rome," and in some cases they believed that it was the bells, on their return, that brought the colored eggs. In rural Austria boys with clappers used to go around to announce the hours since the church tower bells did not strike.

After the services of Maundy Thursday, altars are stripped of all ceremonial objects. The Sacrament is removed to a special receptacle at a distance from the altar. These are preparations for the day of deepest mourning in the entire year.

Sometimes people ask why we call it *Good* Friday when things went so badly on that day. Other names for the day have been Long Friday, Great Friday, and God's Friday. Perhaps our Good Friday is a corruption of the latter, as we now say "Good-bye" when it was once "God be with you."

Many strange customs and superstitions have been associated with the day. In the Old World people believed that clothes washed on Good Friday would be spotted with stains reminiscent of blood. No blacksmith would drive a nail that day because of the nails in the cross. It was traditional, for the same reason, not to drive anything made of iron into the ground on that day.

Good Friday was fortunate for some agriculture, however. It was a lucky day to plant parsley, good also for beans or peas, and a very good day to graft fruit trees. Fishermen considered it unlucky to go fishing, but beekeepers could with good omens move bees. If it rained, you should catch the rain in a bottle because this would cure eye troubles. Breaking dishes was good luck, since some-

how this would bruise Judas. Gypsies would not use water
on Good Friday because of Pilate's washing his hands.

In the fishing community of Brighton, England, all day
long people skipped rope and the day was known as Hand
Rope Day. In England and Holland playing marbles was
a very important tradition. Boys and men played marbles
before they went in, and as soon as they came out of,
church, even if they never played at any other time of the
year. This may have had some relation to the dice-throw-
ing of the Roman soldiers who guarded Jesus on the cross.

The Irish observe what they call "black fast" on Good
Friday, taking no food, only water or tea. In Central Europe only vegetable soup and bread was served at noon,
only cheese and bread at night. Both meals were eaten
standing and in silence. The entire day was somber, the
children's usual games forbidden, no joking, laughing, or
noisy work.

In parts of Europe it was considered fortunate to die on
Good Friday. Those persons who do are said to share in
the privilege of the Good Thief, that of a speedy entry
to Heaven.

In Spanish countries life-size figures of the Crucifixion
are carried in procession. At three in the afternoon in the
church flashing powder is set off to simulate thunder, a
reminder of the storm that raged when Jesus died. Then
a priest climbs a ladder and detaches the body from the
crucifix, leaving a bare cross. The figure of Christ is placed
in a Shrine of the Sepulchre, where people come to pray
all evening.

The Eastern (Orthodox) Church has no statues, only
flat pictures. While no dimensional figure of Christ is in

evidence, a small silver coffin with a cross in it may be honored, or a picture of Christ painted on a winding sheet, surrounded by lights and flowers. The faithful kneel to kiss the cross or the painted figure.

Many churches in this country and abroad conduct services from noon until 3 P.M. in remembrance of the time Jesus was on the Cross. This is called the Service of the Three Hours and was first held in Lima, Peru, in 1732. The custom quickly spread through the Latin countries, went to England from Italy, and thence to the United States. It is carried on in Protestant churches as well as Catholic, and often in union services of several denominations. Usually it consists of brief sermons on the seven last sayings of Christ, alternating with hymns and prayers. Many downtown churches have this type of service, where business people drop in for an hour and slip out during the singing of a hymn. The tradition is practically unknown in France, Canada, and Central Europe. Instead choirs present oratorios based on the "seven last words" on Friday night.

This is often done in America, too. Musical services recounting the Passion story on Good Friday afternoon replaced the liturgical service in Germany after the Reformation. Antonio Scandello, who died in 1580, wrote the first such service, a St. John's Passion. Heinrich Schütz, who lived until 1672, set all four Gospel narratives to music. The best known examples of this music are Bach's *St. John* and *St. Matthew Passions*. The first performance of the *St. John* was on Good Friday, 1723, at Leipzig, but there was no performance of the complete work in this country until 1880, when it was done by the Bach Choir of Bethlehem, Pennsylvania.

Because Judas used the word at the betrayal of Jesus, Syrian and Arab Christians do not use the ordinary greeting *salām 'alaykum*, which means "Peace be with you," from Thursday night until after Easter. They may use the popular "Happy Holiday," or the very devout may say, "The Light of God be with your departed ones."

Fire and water seem to have special significance in Lenten customs, which reach their culmination on Holy Saturday, the Saturday of Mourning. Undoubtedly these are remnants of pagan days, but the significance has changed to have meaning for Christians. In the Austrian Alps on mountain peaks Easter fires which can be seen for great distances glow Saturday night. Young people like to dance, sing Easter hymns, and jump over the fires. Bonfires, called Judas Fires, used to be kindled in the churchyard, burning up the wooden crosses that had fallen or broken from graves. A palm from Palm Sunday was always added to the fire, and sometimes an effigy of Judas was burned.

Latin America, Spain, and Portugal make a great deal of the burning of Judas. Hideous effigies of Judas stuffed with straw and gunpowder are sold from booths all over Mexico City on Good Friday morning. They are hung on ropes stretched from house to house and are hooted at and cursed in vivid Spanish. A few minutes before noon the crowd becomes quiet, listening for the bells from the cathedral. The twelve o'clock bell signals a time of frenzied yelling and excitement as the Judas figures are cut down and thrown into the flames of fires, where they explode with the loud noise and the acrid smell of gunpowder. With the yells of defiance there is rejoicing. These people get a lot out of their systems in a harmless way by venting their

rage at evil on the effigies. There is little that a poor work-
man can do about the grinding misery of his poverty and
existence, but on this one day he can register his opinion
about all that is bad in the world.

St. Patrick is supposed to have originated the Blessing
of the Easter Fire to overcome the effect of the heathen
Spring Fire rites. Chief remnant of this is the lighting of
the Paschal candle, a particularly large candle, sometimes
on a floor candlestick, which remains lighted during Mass
from Saturday night through Whitsuntide, representing
the Risen Christ. In some homes where vigil lights are kept
before a crucifix or images of the saints, these are extin-
guished on Saturday and relighted on Easter. The fire
brands to light the candles and other fires in the house used
to be hurried from the church after the priest had blessed
them.

In America the only vestige of the Easter vigil, which at
one time was all of Saturday night, seems to be a Saturday
evening service. In the early days of the Christian era baptisms were performed during the night vigil. A large basin
was placed outside the church, and both the bishop and
the person he was baptizing stepped into it. Then the newly
baptized were anointed and dressed in flowing garments of
white linen which they wore all through Easter week. At
dawn they received communion for the first time.

At the Church of the Holy Sepulchre in Jerusalem, the
Greek Orthodox Patriarch of the Holy City hands a burning taper out from the tomb in the church. People wait
outside the gates with candles which are lighted from his,
with great jubilation. This is a custom which has been
kept since the twelfth century.

In Spain the celebration of Easter really comes on Saturday with the organ crashing like thunder and a purple curtain dramatically parted to reveal the altar. Then the organ plays triumphantly, bells peal, the choir sings "Gloria in Excelsis," the Sacrament returns to the high altar, and they celebrate the Triumph of Easter. Sunday isn't a holy day—everybody goes to the bull fight.

The Eastern Church has Midnight Mass on Saturday with the church almost dark as the people gather. Suddenly the lights come on, either with candles lighted from a central one or dramatically done with electric light, and the priest says joyfully, "Christ is risen," to which the people respond, "He is risen indeed." This same greeting is used throughout the next days of celebration. After the service people go visiting to friends' homes to wish them a Happy Easter.

In Protestant churches Saturday is a quiet day, and there is usually no activity in the church except for the arrangement of flowers for the early service on Easter morning. It is still a solemn day with the thoughts of Good Friday still fresh in the memory.

Almost everyone accepts the cross as the symbol of Christianity. Just as Jewish military chaplains are identified by tiny tablets-of-the-law, Protestant, Roman Catholic, and Orthodox chaplains are identified by a cross. Many churches are topped by the symbol, and most others display the cross inside the building. Some churches prefer the figure of the dying Christ on the cross, others an empty cross, sometimes colored gold and quite elaborate. The handle on the top of the communion set is often in the shape of the cross, the symbol decorates the baptismal font, the pulpit chairs, often pews, most stained-glass windows, sometimes the candlesticks, often the pulpit hangings, sometimes the minister's stole. In this country we are often in danger of thinking of the cross as only a symbol and not as a historic instrument used to produce a horrible death which was considered necessary punishment for the worst criminals.

Today the cross is honored. Even a person of another religion would not be likely to desecrate a cross. Cemeteries abound with them. In military graveyards the pattern made by the even row of crosses is often photographed because of its beauty. Crosses are placed at danger spots in the mountains where people have died from accidents. This brings us closer to the original meaning of the cross than do the gold or jeweled ones hung from chains around the necks of attractive women. A cross means death—and, originally, a shameful one.

Newer churches often use rough wooden crosses, rather than the smooth gilt ones of earlier years, in an attempt at getting closer to the original meaning. One church saves the trunk of the Christmas tree and lashes it into a cross for Holy Week. One of the most moving of the religious displays at the New York World's Fair in 1964–65 was the Coventry Cross, brought over from Coventry Cathedral in England for display in the garden at the Protestant and Orthodox Pavilion. The cross, a very simple one, is made of charred logs from the bombed-out cathedral. But it tells a story of suffering and of sacrifice. And somehow, though it speaks of destruction, it is a symbol of hope.

It is interesting that the pictures and writings on the walls of the catacombs, where the early Christians buried their dead and met secretly, do not include the cross as a symbol. To them the disgrace was too recent. It would be rather like our using a drawing of an electric chair. Some of these early Christians, too, died on crosses. For three hundred years the cross was not an element of worship. The earliest use of it in art shows a triumphant Christ coming out of the tomb carrying a cross. Through the years we have added significance to the symbol and varied its form. The danger is that we may rivet our attention on the instrument of death rather than on the meaning of the event.

It is not the cross that is the Saviour—but Christ. Perhaps our veneration of the cross somehow mitigates for us the suffering. But Jesus knew that the suffering was a necessary part of the joy. Christians were told later, "Count it all joy when ye fall into divers temptations," or as the New English Bible has it: "Whenever you have to face trials of many kinds, count yourselves supremely happy." We have not known complete joy until we have known the joy that is to be found in the midst of suffering.

3 · *The Joy of*
Continuity

MANY people in America are proud that their ancestors were among the earliest colonists. Belonging to the Daughters of the American Revolution or Sons of the Old Dominion is considered a great privilege. Some of us whose parents or grandparents came to this country as immigrants at a later date are just as proud of them for undergoing the great adventure of transferring to these shores. We like to look back on our forebears and find out what made them do the things they did. Most Americans like to recall the vigor of pioneer times, the poignant tragedy of our Civil War, our growth as an industrial nation, and

such feats as the completion of the transcontinental rail-
way, the Panama Canal, Lindbergh's solo flight to Paris.
We like to think of ourselves in the succession of those
hardy souls on the frontier, the great statesmen, generals,
achievers—people like Thomas Edison, Charles Steinmetz,
George Washington Carver, Clara Barton. We like to think
of ourselves as in the stream of an exciting history which
is America.

Christians are also part of a history—a larger history that
involves the dealings of God with man. This recorded
history takes us back to the earliest Books of Moses, or the
Book of Job—which of course takes us back to the people
through whom, we are told, God first chose to reveal Himself. In the light of all that Christians owe the Jews in the
way of beginnings and of how much the two groups have
in common, it is incomprehensible that there should be
anti-Semitism among those who call themselves Christian.

Christians need to remind themselves often that Jesus
was Jewish, His mother Mary was Jewish, Joseph of Naza-
reth, through whom Jesus' legal descent is counted, was
Jewish; both Mary and Joseph traced back to David, who
was king during Israel's golden age. Paul, who is called
the Apostle to the Gentiles, was proud of his Jewish heritage and continually reminded the early Christians of their
debt to all that had gone before. "When the fulness of the
time was come," Paul writes to the new Christians in the
area of Galatia, "God sent forth his Son, made of a woman,
made under the law," which was his way of emphasizing
the Jewishness of the One Christians call Saviour.

Most Christians accept Abraham and Jacob as spiritual
forebears and are usually quite surprised that Muslims do,

too. If the Arabs, most of whom are Muhammadan, are physically descended from Abraham through Ishmael, they have even more right than we to be considered children of Abraham. This is a heritage we can afford to share.

How exciting to be a part, though certainly a come-lately part, of God's working in the history of man. The more we learn about the Old Testament and about Judaism, the more we as Christians feel ourselves fitting into history.

Everyone needs to feel a part of something, to feel needed. Those who accept Jesus Christ as Saviour are sharing in the great stream of God's revelation of Himself to human beings. Let us learn as much as we can about our heritage.

The celebration of Passover starts on the eve of the fourteenth day of Nisan, which is usually near Easter. Passover commemorates the events recorded in the twelfth chapter of Exodus, when the firstborn of the Israelites were kept safe while the Egyptian firstborn sons and animals died. This gave the Israelite slaves the opportunity they had been waiting for to leave Egypt and they set off quickly after eating a hurried meal of roast lamb while standing up. Today age-old ceremonies commemorate this ancient stand against tyranny, and remind Jews that liberty cannot be inherited, but must be guarded and fought for by each generation.

Passover is celebrated for seven days in Israel, but in the United States and some Western European countries it lasts eight days. In this country many Jews hold Seders the first two nights, and on the last two days special synagogue services are held. Since Passover is so closely connected with home and family, those who are living in cities where they have no relatives are often invited to share the Seder with

a family. The custom gives special significance to the question asked by Peter and John, "Where wilt thou that we prepare for thee to eat the Passover?" Jesus had no home in Jerusalem, but a place was provided by a friend.

Often called the Feast of Unleavened Bread, the Passover is characterized by the eating of matzos, a form of cracker, instead of bread made with yeast or other leavening agent. Just before the holiday there is a great cleaning of the house to ensure that no particle of leavening or any grain that may become fermented (chometz) is left. Then, before the Passover meal can be prepared, the father inspects the house and declares it free of chometz. New dishes, or a set kept only for Passover, are used at this time, and foods must be certified "kosher for Passover" by a rabbinical authority. This means that they have not come in contact with a leavening agent during the preparing and packaging.

The Seder is celebrated with ceremonial foods reminiscent of the occasion when the ancestors left Egypt. Questions are asked about the meaning of the day, with the youngest child asking and the father or the eldest family member leading the company in answering. The essential form for this ceremony has not varied much over the years; a book called "Passover" Haggada, the story of the Exodus, gives directions, prayers, and hymns for the ritual.

At sunset as the holy day begins the head of the family usually goes to the synagogue where the festival evening prayer is recited, while at home last-minute preparations are completed for the Seder. Often he wears a white gown or at least a white cap and white socks, because a heavenly visitor is expected. His chair at the dinner table has a white cushion, sometimes embroidered with a crown. The table has been set with special care, with a clean linen cloth and candlesticks. The ceremonial foods are set out on plates in a prescribed order: three matzos, wrapped in a special napkin so they do not touch each other, representing the High Priests, the Levites, and the lay people; a bunch of parsley or other green herbs, symbolizing the hyssop which was used to mark the doorposts of the Israelites; a little horse-radish to represent bitter herbs, symbolic of their bitter life in Egypt; some saltwater or vinegar, representing the tears they shed; a roasted egg and a shankbone of lamb or other meat, in remembrance of the Passover lamb and the sacrifice offered on Passover eve in the Temple before it was de-stroyed; and haroseth, a mixture of apples, nuts, and wine, representing the mortar used to make bricks during their slavery in Egypt. On the table also are small cups of wine, reminding the participants of God's four statements to re-deem Israel, and a larger wine cup for Elijah, the heavenly visitor, for whom a place has been set at the table.

The housewife lights the candles, saying a prayer as she does so. The head of the family says the Kiddush, or blessing over wine, then drinks the wine while reclining on his side. He washes his hands and, taking the parsley, dips it into the saltwater and says: "Blesed art thou, O Lord our God, King of the universe, who createst the fruit of the earth." Then he breaks the middle matzo into two unequal parts and places the larger part, the afikomen or dessert, beneath the cushion on his seat. He uncovers the matzos, takes the shank bone and the egg off the dish, lifts the dish and says: "Lo, this is the bread of affliction, which our ancestors ate in the land of Egypt; let all those who are hungry enter and eat thereof; and all who are in need come and celebrate the Passover. . . ." The wine cups are filled a second time and the youngest child present asks: "Wherefore is this night different from all other nights? On all other nights we may eat leavened or unleavened bread, but on this night only unleavened bread; on all other nights we may eat any species of herbs, but on this night only bitter herbs; on all other nights we do not dip even once, but on this night twice; on all other nights we eat and drink either sitting or reclining, but on this night we all eat reclining."

The ceremony which follows is a reply to the question, and relates the story of the slavery in Egypt, the Exodus, the parables, and the commentary by sages in the centuries that followed. Prayers and songs are included, in some of which the entire company joins.

Everyone tastes the bitter herbs and the haroseth, and has a piece of the broken egg, memorializing the destruction of the Temple. After this, the actual meal is served, and this is a joyous time of happy conversation and good eating. The meal might consist of borscht (beet soup), roast chicken, sponge cake, fruit, and tea. When the meal is finished the head of the family takes the half matzo from its hiding place under the cushion and gives everyone a piece to eat. All wash their hands, and grace is said. The ceremony continues with the drinking of the two remaining cups of wine, the opening of the door for the heavenly visitor, prayers and blessings, finishing with the Hallel, or psalms of praise.

The next seven or eight days of the festival are observed by using "Kosher for Passover" foods.

Christians and Jews share an interest in the first Passover when the blood on the doorposts meant safety for the first-born of the family within. The symbol of the lamb, killed so the people could be free, is particularly significant to Christians. Also, it was the time when Jesus was keeping Passover with His disciples—or possibly the night of preparation before the actual Passover—that He introduced the Lord's Supper, which has become our Communion Service, or the Eucharist. So for historic as well as symbolic reasons, there is interest in the holiday for Christians.

In most European languages the word for Easter is derived from Pascha, the Greek word for Passover. This probably accounts for the mistranslation in the King James Version in Acts 12:4 where the word "Easter" appears: "intending after Easter to bring him forth to the people." All other translations use "Passover."

In the early days the celebration of Christ's resurrection followed the Jewish custom of figuring Passover, which is related to the Hebrew lunar calendar. But it was thought best for the celebrations not to coincide, so the Council of Nicea in A.D. 325 decided that Easter should be observed on the first Sunday after the full moon that appears on or following the spring equinox. Since the equinox is March 21, this meant that Easter could never be before March 22 or after April 25. In 1943 we had a late Easter—April 25—the only time in this century when it will be on that date.

A great deal of sentiment has been in favor of stabilizing the date so it does not move around from year to year. A number of church bodies—British Methodist, Presbyterian World Alliance, and some Roman Catholic groups have endorsed the idea, and the World Council of Churches is studying the desirability of fixing a common date for Easter throughout Christendom. The Eastern Orthodox churches usually have a different date from churches in the West, because they use the Julian rather than the Gregorian calendar.

Many Christians see significance for themselves in the ceremony of the Seder. A number of Protestant churches have been holding a Passover meal during Holy Week, particularly on Maundy Thursday, to feel a little closer to the mood of Jesus' last days on earth. This is a time when Christians can learn from their Jewish friends and neighbors. Most Jews will be happy to describe the ceremony and explain its significance.

A Presbyterian minister has commented to his congregation that Jewish religious holidays are much more enthusiastically celebrated in many Jewish homes than are Christian holidays in Christian homes. He feels the reason is that they have kept the solemnity and festivity together, while Christians have separated them. You go to church for late solemn service on Christmas Eve, and the funtime is at home when packages are opened the next morning. Easter in the church is all lilies and alleluias, but the real festivity is the egg hunting and the chocolate rabbits that await the children after church. There is much to be said for a happy home festival full of laughter and gaiety, yet in which all are reminded of the sacred events for which the day is celebrated.

Children need roots; they need to know about their ancestors so that they may eventually learn who they are. Christian children need to learn about the pioneers of faith —Abraham, who followed God not knowing where he was being led; the leaders of the rebellion—Moses, who led the people out of slavery and helped form them into a nation; the poets—David, the "sweet singer of Israel"; the philosophers—Job, who discovered that God was there; the teachers, the politicians, the activists, the improvers—and the failures. Passover is an opportunity for putting our spiritual history into focus, for finding our place in the scheme of things, for remembering. It is fortunate that it falls so near Eastertime, that we may share in the remembrance and may experience the joy of continuity.

4. *The Joy of New Beginnings*

THERE is excitement in newness. Who can resist the charm of fuzzy chicks only a day or two out of the shell or lambs on wobbly legs frolicking in the sunshine or the wonder of a brilliant tulip which such a short time ago was an ugly brown bulb? Who does not feel more confident and more at peace with the world when wearing smart new clothes? Who has not caught his breath at the marvel of a sunrise or of the first crocus showing through the snow

Easter is many things. First of all it is the commemoration of the day when Jesus Christ rose from the dead.

From our vantage point centuries later, it is difficult to put ourselves in the position of the disciples and others who loved Jesus. What hopelessness must have settled over them that Friday evening! The Leader who was going to take them into a glorious new way of life, perhaps even overthrow the government, was now lying dead in a tomb. They had been so busy telling people about the Kingdom He was starting and helping the suffering that they were totally unprepared. There hadn't even been money for a burial plot, but fortunately a well-wisher had come forward and offered his own tomb, and that was where the King was now lying. It had all been so hurried, because sunset was approaching and people were not buried on the Sabbath. So they had quickly wrapped the body in a winding sheet, set it in the tomb, and pushed the big stone back over the opening. No embalming spices, no ceremony— what a way to bury a king! And where was the Kingdom now?

It was the saddest Sabbath day of their lives. One wonders what lesson was read in the synagogue that Passover Sabbath. Probably those who had been close to Jesus were afraid to attend, lest they be arrested and suffer His fate. Doubtless they were staying out of sight, hiding, perhaps, in homes of friends.

But early the next morning several of the women started for the tomb with spices to complete a proper burial. As they went they discussed the problem of the stone—the heavy circular slab that rolled in a groove just outside the opening of the cavelike tomb. As they approached, they saw that the stone was already rolled aside; they would have no difficulty getting inside. But the solution to their problem did not bring them joy. They shuddered. Who could have pushed the stone? Surely no friend. They were so early, no one else in their group would have been there yet. It must have been an enemy. Just as with so many of us, they were certain the worst had happened.

What a surprise when they reached the tomb! No signs of vandalism, but instead men in shining garments telling them, "He is not here: for He is risen." So they rushed off to tell the good news. Of course the disciples couldn't believe the words of foolish women. Peter and John had to see for themselves. They saw the linen cloths which had been wrapped around the body, still in the same shape but with the body gone. This was evidence to them of a miracle.

Mary Magdalene seemed to be the hardest to convince. The angels, the graveclothes—nothing stilled her grief until a familiar voice spoke her name. Then she, too, knew that the Lord was alive.

In the afternoon two disciples on the road to Emmaus were joined by a stranger who discussed theology with them, bringing Old Testament Scripture up to date by relating it to the recent events in Jerusalem. Slowly they began to realize that this Jesus must really have been the Messiah promised so long ago and that these were things that had to happen to the Messiah. Suddenly, the stranger was gone. They rushed back to the city to find eleven of the disciples gathered in a room discussing these strange happenings. Eagerly they recounted their adventures and without warning, there He was with them—Jesus, the One they all knew and loved, recognizable though different. "Then," the account says, "were the disciples glad."

The gladness has echoed through the centuries. This is what makes Easter: the angels' words, "He is risen," and the echo in our consciousness, "He is risen indeed" or "I, too, have experienced that He is alive."

Each year at Eastertime hundreds of Christians travel to Jerusalem to try to get the feel of the Passion, to "spend Easter where Easter began." On Good Friday throngs of the faithful go sadly down the Via Dolorosa, supposedly the path Jesus walked, carrying His cross to Calvary. Border restrictions are lifted to allow Christians living in Israel to visit the historic sites in old Jerusalem which are in Jordan; there is visiting back and forth between families and friends, something that is not allowed the rest of the year.

For many persons, the Church of the Holy Sepulchre is the exact spot where Christ was buried, with the ancient church built over the cave. Many Protestants find the Garden Tomb, under the hill which is referred to as Gordon's

Calvary, more satisfying and nearer their idea of the actual tomb. The hill above does look like a skull with two small caves resembling eye sockets, a ridge that suggests a nose, and an opening below. Over three hundred tombs have been excavated in Jerusalem, but this one is thought by a great many archaeologists and Biblical scholars to be most like the type of tomb which would have been Joseph of Arimathea's. Whether this is the actual tomb perhaps does not matter; the quiet spirit of the place is conducive to meditation about what happened that wonderful morning.

The garden is maintained by a private English society which installed the Rev. S. J. Mattar, a Christian Arab refugee from Israel, as custodian. If the visitor asks for it, one of the Mattar family will give him a tour and lecture, but one is also free to wander through alone. The shaded garden with the open tomb carved out of the rock, the hill that looks like a skull just above, all turn the mind to the happenings of that first Easter. It is quite a contrast to the busy, ornate Church of the Holy Sepulchre.

Early Easter morning the services begin at the Garden Tomb. Touring groups of Americans and English interrupt their sightseeing for a service at the tomb, some beginning as early as four in the morning—before it is actually light. For many, this is the highlight of a spring tour to the Holy Lands. All through the day groups will come to conduct their own service there, with assistance from Mr. Mattar.

Early morning services are characteristic of Easter in America. Often called an Easter dawn or sunrise service, usually it does not get underway until after the sun is well up. The first spot in continental United States which is hit by the Easter sun is Cadillac Mountain in Acadia Na-

tional Park, just outside Bar Harbor, Maine. Every year
a group of hardy young people and some adults shiver in
the cool morning sunlight and raise their alleluias in the
often frosty air. Maine can be chilly even in June—and
particularly in March or April.

At least nineteen national parks have Easter sunrise services. In Aspen, Colorado, worshipers travel by ski lift. Red
Rocks Amphitheater outside Denver was built particularly
for these services, though it is used now for concerts as well.
Garden of the Gods in Colorado Springs has a famous
dawn service that has long been carried on network radio,
as has the Grand Canyon, Soldier Field in Chicago, Cathe-
dral of the Pines in Rindge, New Hampshire, and Yosemite
National Park and the Hollywood Bowl in California.
There is a service at Lincoln's birthplace in Hodgenville,
Kentucky, another on the steps of the Capitol in Salt Lake
City. The service at the Tomb of the Unknown Soldier in
Arlington National Cemetery, near Washington, D.C., at-
tracts people from great distances. The last sunrise service
of the morning is held in the crater of a passive volcano at
Punchbowl National Memorial Cemetery outside Hono-
lulu.

Nearly every town and city in the United States has
several such early services, usually in a spot of beauty out-
of-doors. One well-known indoor service is held at New
York City's mammoth Radio City Music Hall, sponsored
by the city's Protestant Council. But Central Park also is
the scene of a sunrise service, as are many smaller parks
around the city. In Columbus, Ohio, the Conservatory at
the Botanic Gardens provides an outdoor jungle setting
with warm comfort. At Tampa, Florida, where the cold

morning air is no problem, a special feature of one service is the releasing of thirty-three white pigeons. In Lawton, Oklahoma, a six-hour pageant from midnight to dawn, showing the life of Christ, is climaxed by the enactment of the Resurrection. The project began in 1926 with a group from the Congregational Church.

The claim for the first Easter sunrise service in this coun-

try is made by Spanish explorers who conducted a service
on their ship anchored off California on Easter of 1609.
But more probably the custom was brought by the Moravians who settled in Winston-Salem, North Carolina, in
1773. The Moravian Easter customs, still kept in such
strong settlements as Bethlehem, Pennsylvania, and Winston-Salem, and even in tiny Gnaddenhutten, Ohio, are
most picturesque and in keeping with the spirit of the day.

Young people are up at 3:30 A.M., loosening up their
trombones. While it is still quite dark they begin playing
Easter hymns from the belfry of the church, with another
group answering from the parsonage steps. This antiphonal
brass choir music and playing through the dark streets of
the town goes on until nearly daylight. The people, aroused
by the music, hurry before 5:00 to the church, where the
only illumination comes from a lighted cross surrounded
by palms on the altar. When it is time for the service to
begin the minister rushes into the darkened church and
shouts, "The Lord is risen!" The congregation rises to its
feet to respond, "He is risen indeed!" much in the same
manner as in the Greek Orthodox church. Lights come on
and a ritual service follows. Then the entire congregation
walks to the graveyard where another brief service is held,
and they return to the church for breakfast, which has
been prepared by a men's group.

Easter sunrise services are supposed to have originated
in the Middle Ages when very early on Easter morning
joyful voices, the boom of cannon, and the clanging of
bells announced the happy news, Christ is risen! Even older
traditions of dancing to welcome the sun or getting up to
watch the angels dance existed in Europe. Elderly people

in France used to say that the first few persons to see the sun on Easter morning would see angels dancing in the rays extending into the dark sky. In England they thought the lamb with banner was visible in the very center of the sun when it first rose. Just as the winter solstice is referred to as the Birth of the Sun, so the vernal equinox is called Dawn of the Sun. There has always been a connection between spring and sunrise.

Easter is also a joyful greeting. How did people greet each other on Easter morning before it was called Easter? "Alleluia, the Lord is risen" was used generally in early medieval times. In some cases the first person would say, "Christ is truly risen" (in Latin, of course), and the second would respond, "Thanks be to God."

The Orthodox still use the greeting, "Christ is risen," and the answer, "He is risen indeed," even in Russia and the Ukraine. The custom was adopted by many Chinese Christians, too. A Polish greeting is "A joyful alleluia to you!"

Baptism has always had a connection with Easter, particularly in the Eastern Church. In many Protestant churches it used to be the custom to baptize infants on Easter, but in most cases this is now done the week before or after. Possibly our custom of wearing new clothes on this holiday comes from the baptisms conducted in the early church. The new converts were given white garments in the flowing Roman style to put on immediately after their baptism on Easter Day. This signified joy and new life and they wore the white robes all week, which gave it the name of White Week.

Today we dress in our best, usually new clothes, to go to church or to walk around the streets. The Easter "parade" has been greatly criticized as an evidence of vanity, and no doubt it often is, though it has religious origins. When the service was over in European churches, the congregation used to take an Easter walk through the fields or an open place, all dressed in their good new clothes. Sometimes a candle or crucifix led the procession and there was singing of hymns. In certain sections of Germany and Austria richly decorated horses were part of the procession of Easter, ridden by their young farmer owners. After the Reformation the Easter walk lost its religious character, but it remains in such highly publicized events as the Fifth Avenue Easter Parade in New York City.

New clothing has always been important to spring festivals, even in pagan times. It even has a connection with romance. At one time a man would send a girl to whom he was attracted a pair of gloves on Easter Eve. If she wore them to church on Easter it was an acceptance of his proposal of marriage. Probably then gloves did not come in as many colors as today. Imagine the consternation of a young woman whose Easter outfit was a carefully matched costume of yellows suddenly receiving a pair of red gloves —if she really liked the young man who sent them.

Perhaps even more important than new clothes as a symbol of Easter are the spring flowers, particularly those grown from bulbs—daffodils, narcissus, tulips, Easter lilies, hyacinths. The imagery of new life and beauty coming from a brown, dead-looking bulb is easy to understand. Perhaps this is the best explanation of resurrection for a small child.

Daffodils which grow wild in the English countryside are called Lent lilies and are in bloom in much of the world during the Lenten season. Several species are native to the Holy Land. Actually a daffodil is a narcissus, though we usually consider this a white flower. The narcissus has long had a place in mythology, supposed to have been brought forth by Earth at the request of Adonis to snare the flower-like Persephone. A hundred blossoms burst from the roots of the plant at the girl's feet, making Earth and Sky and Sea glad at the scent. Persephone was enchanted and stretched forth her hands to take the flower, whereupon Earth

opened and she was seized and carried below. The gods' unusual methods of securing wives has not diminished our pleasure in this fragrant spring flower.

Tulips grow wild in the Near East, though not the large Dutch variety usually grown here in the springtime. It is one of the plants referred to there as lily of the field, along with the anemone. This latter flower, somewhat more fragile in appearance, grows in wild profusion in Israel and Jordan, coloring the fields purple, pink, white, and red. It has long been associated with the Passion. The anemone, or wind flower, is common in Europe, even in the high mountain meadows of Switzerland. It is believed to have been brought back from the Holy Land during the Crusades. Seeds of the flower were included in the holy soil which was brought to Pisa in Italy, where the flowers grew and became native. From there they spread all over Europe.

A form of hyacinth grows wild in the Holy Land, as does the cyclamen. The latter has been dedicated to the Virgin Mary by Roman Catholics because of the spot of color—the drop of blood—in the heart of the flower.

The plant most often connected with Easter—the beautiful waxy white Easter lily—is not a spring flower and is unknown in the Near East. The lily that is featured by painters and sculptors in religious art is the Madonna Lily, which blooms in early summer. This is not easily forced and so is unavailable at Eastertime. In the 1880's Mrs. Sargent, an amateur gardener who was visiting in Bermuda, brought back to Philadelphia some bulbs of a beautiful white lily she found there. They grew nicely and she showed the flowers proudly to her friends. A Philadelphia nurseryman, William K. Harris, introduced the lilies to the florist trade under the name *Lilium Harrisi* and featured them at flower shows. Within ten years they had become an essential Easter flower, and large shipments of lilies went from Bermuda to the United States and England each year.

Actually the lilies were not natives of Bermuda, but were introduced there by a missionary who was returning from Japan to the United States. He had admired the lilies he found growing on islands south of Japan and brought along bulbs of the blunderbuss or gun lily, as it was called. Several bulbs were left with a friend whom he visited in Bermuda and they grew very well in the ideal conditions there. Before long they had spread all over the island.

Our Easter lilies are now mostly homegrown, however. A serious blight attacked the Bermuda lilies in the late 1920's, so American growers attempted again to find a strain that would grow in our climate. In 1931 the Croft lily, named for a grower in Oregon, was introduced and is now the one commonly called Easter lily. Today California and the Pacific Northwest furnish most of the lily bulbs that are forced by the million all over the country each Easter.

A rather uncommon plant associated with Easter is called the resurrection plant or the Palestine tumbleweed. The Jews call it rose of Jericho. The plant dies and rolls up like a ball, apparently dead, but when placed in water it resumes its natural form and begins to grow again. This may be the "stubble before the wind" referred to in Job 21:18 and Psalm 83:13.

The early-flowering trees are often included as Easter flowers, depending on the date of the holiday and the weather. The earliest tree to show color in northern woods is usually the redbud, also called the Judas tree because it resembles a species that grows wild in the Holy Land. The dogwood is another blossoming tree growing in the eastern part of the United States that has a connection with Easter. Almost everyone has heard the legend which has arisen rather recently based on the markings of the flower. The tree is unknown in Bible lands, but the story goes that once it was as tall and heavy as other forest trees and was chosen to be used for Jesus' cross. The use to which it was put so distressed the tree that Jesus, in pity, decreed that it should no longer grow tall enough to be used for a cross, but that its blossoms should be in the shape of a cross with a rusty-red thumb print in each petal and a crown of thorns in the center. It is an unusual reminder of the Passion story.

Animals as well as flowers are used as symbols of the Resurrection. We are used to the chicken, the rabbit, and the lamb, but the lion, the whale, and the butterfly also have been associated with Easter.

The lion became a resurrection symbol because of mistaken zoology. There was a tradition that the lion cub is born dead, and after three days the father lion breathes on the cub and it receives life. However, the strength and majesty of the lion, its association with kingship, and the reference to Christ as "the lion of the tribe of Judah," have made it an acceptable symbol.

It is easy to see why the whale is an Easter symbol. Jonah was as good as dead while he was in the great fish, popularly referred to as a whale, and when he was tossed out on the land, it was as someone coming to life from the dead. When the scribes and Pharisees asked Jesus for a sign, He said: "There shall no sign be given...but the sign of the prophet Jonas; For as Jonas was three days and three nights in the whale's belly: so shall the Son of man be three days and three nights in the heart of the earth." We don't know whether people really understand that He was speaking about his death and resurrection here, but undoubtedly the disciples remembered it later, or at least Matthew who recorded the statement did.

The butterfly is not around at Eastertime but is sometimes used as a symbol, nevertheless. The reason is the remarkable relation of its life cycle to man's total life. First

there is the caterpillar which stays close to the ground, reminding one of man's life on earth. Then there is the dor-
mant stage in the chrysalis or cocoon; we sometimes speak
of being wrapped in the cocoon of death. But finally a
beautiful creature, which soars toward the sky comes forth
from the cocoon, one we consider a much higher form of
life. This speaks of a better life beyond the grave about
which we know very little from the earth side.

One animal symbol has never been seen but has had a
profound effect upon literature—the phoenix. The oldest-
known bird of mythology, it was already a symbol of immortality in many countries in the days of Job. The early
Christians revived it and used it as their own. The myth of
the phoenix is that it lived as long as five hundred years;
then, when it began to feel age, it collected branches from
spice trees for a funeral pyre. Somehow by reflecting the
sun's rays and fanning with its wing, it set itself on fire and
burned up. Nine days later, the phoenix rose from its own

ashes, coming out of an egg it had deposited there before death.

Of course the lamb is an obvious symbol of Jesus' Passion. It was early in His ministry that John the Baptist pointed to Jesus one day and exclaimed, "Behold the Lamb of God which taketh away the sin of the world." He repeated the statement the next day with the result that two of John's disciples left him to follow Jesus. After the cross, the lamb

is the most important symbol in Christianity. Very quickly after the Crucifixion Christ was identified as the One whom the Paschal Lamb foreshadowed, and all the lambs used in sacrifices. The Book of Revelation refers to a Lamb who stood on Mount Zion, "the Lamb slain from the foundation of the world."

The ecclesiastical symbol of Easter shows the lamb carrying a banner bearing a red cross. Wax lambs were distributed by the pastor to parishioners in Finland. They were thought to have protective powers. In some places gold or silver lambs are worn on chains as charms. Cakes baked in the shape of a lamb are popular in Italy and the United States, perhaps originating in Czechoslovakia. Spun-sugar lambs delight the children of Sicily at Eastertime.

While live lambs are sometimes seen in Christmas displays, we do not seem to use them at Easter. It used to be considered lucky to meet a lamb, particularly at the Easter season. The reasoning behind this was the belief that the Devil could not take the form of a lamb, though he could appear as an angel of light or a roaring lion or anything else. Any lamb which crossed your path was sure to be on the right side.

Even the donkey has its place in the symbolism of the Easter season, as the animal on which Jesus rode into Jerusalem in triumphal procession. The humble beast was symbolic at the time of Jesus' identification with the common people, of His peacefulness, since He did not ride a war horse, and of His willingness to use unorthodox methods. Even then the ass was the subject of jokes and known as a very stubborn animal. Many imaginative stories have tried to link this donkey to the one that supposedly carried Mary to Bethlehem. One suggests that this may have been the grandson of the former donkey.

Easter is a rabbit, for some children. Nobody knows for sure where the Easter bunny came from. He seems to be all over, though in Europe he is actually the hare, which has shorter ears, longer hind legs, and a different skull from the rabbit. Besides, European rabbits are born blind, underground, and live in burrows. Hares are born with eyes open and always live aboveground. Because rabbits have five or six litters a year they are considered a fertility symbol, but there is no definite trace to any pagan fertility rites involving rabbits or hares.

The hare is supposed to be a symbol of the moon, according to Egyptian legends. Some people find a connection in the fact that the date of Easter is determined by the moon. The church has never accepted the rabbit as a religious symbol, though a recent writer has found some identification in the fact that the European rabbit lives in a burrow, which could be considered a picture of a tomb, then rises from it to bound over hill and field as we shall someday rise from the dead with great joy.

As a folk custom probably the bunny is the most important symbol of the Easter season, at least to children. Each year parents have difficulty explaining why a rabbit should be bringing colored hen's eggs and why *he* is laying eggs at all.

The earliest mention of Easter eggs and the Easter rabbit is in a late-sixteenth-century German book: "Do not worry if the bunny escapes you; should we miss his eggs then we shall cook the nest." In a German book dated 1682 the bunny lays eggs and hides them in the garden, but already it is referred to as an old fable. They thought the bunny laid red eggs on Maundy Thursday and the other colors on Easter Eve. Probably it is Germany to which we owe the folk tradition of the Easter bunny as we do the favorite tradition of Christmas, the decorated Christmas tree.

The custom came to this country with the German settlers who arrived in the 1770's, and provided children one of their greatest pleasures. Youngsters prepared the nests in hopes of finding colored eggs on Easter morning, though there was some question about it since it hinged on their having been good. Nests made of hats or bonnets or fancy paper boxes were put in secluded spots because the rabbit was believed to be quite shy. Some families put gifts by the children's table settings at Easter breakfast or on windowsills instead of the hidden nests.

Hungarian and German children traditionally find a hare in the basket of eggs. In Panama it is the *conejo* or painted rabbit who brings Easter eggs. Children of Yugoslavia search the hay for the eggs; apparently the hare makes his own nest.

Pennsylvania Dutch children are delighted with Easter cake made of bread dough formed into the shape of a rabbit with a raisin eye and a colored hard-boiled egg beneath the bunny's tail. The first Easter bunnies of pastry and sugar were made in southern Germany in the early 1800's and now are found all over. In this country the chocolate rabbit is a must for the Easter basket.

It is easy to see why fuzzy chicks and ducklings found their way into Easter baskets, because both chicken and duck eggs are used, though this is an American and not a European custom. Stuffed toys shaped like chicks, which are popular with small children here, are not common elsewhere, though the bunny toy is universal.

Roosters have long had a relation to Easter. In most Latin countries they are made in ceramic; in Mexico tin is used. The red or bright blue wooden rooster of Sweden has become quite popular here as a kitchen accessory. The cock,

which crowed during the trial of Jesus and reminded Peter of Jesus' words about his denial, is a religious symbol. Occasionally a church will have a gilt cock high atop its steeple, not only as a weathervane but a reminder of that infamous night. Cockfighting used to be a popular sport during Shrovetide in England, although it is forbidden today.

The hen, too, has an Easter significance—it was to the protectiveness of a hen that Jesus compared His compassion for the capital city He loved, as every Jew loves it. "O Jerusalem, Jerusalem, thou that killest the prophets, and stonest them which are sent unto thee, how often would I have gathered thy children together, even as a hen gathereth her chickens under her wings, and ye would not!" Just how much they would not is proved by what happened there during His last week.

Of course the hen is the source for most of our gaily colored Easter eggs and deserves a mention on that score. The egg is perhaps the best-known symbol of new life that we have, and it has been known to almost every people through the ages. The shell is compared to a tomb in which is imprisoned the germ of life until the day the shell is broken and the new life enters the world.

The egg has been the subject of philosophy. It was Thomas Aquinas in the thirteenth century who first asked the question heard so often since concerning which came first, the chicken or the egg.

The egg is involved in mythology with the origin of the earth, a symbol of creation, in ancient Egypt and India. Hindus and the earlier Phoenicians believed that a great egg split apart to form heaven and earth. The Egyptian myth has the World-Egg coming from the god of the sky and the god of the earth. This egg produces the Sun-Bird who becomes supreme over both earth and sky.

A common theme in Hindu art is a swan, or sometimes a gander, floating on the waters of chaos with the World-Egg beneath him. The bird is a symbol of Brahma, the supreme essence or soul of the universe. This reminds us of Genesis where we are told that "the Spirit of God moved upon [or brooded over] the face of the waters." And the symbol of the Spirit is the dove.

The Phoenicians also associated the egg with the moon, which they visualized as floating in liquid space that must have been the source of the spring rains that brought new life to the earth. The Druids had a special regard for serpent eggs and held a religious rite in which the people danced in a ring around a huge pile of eggs. This was supposed to represent a chain without end, or the circle of eternity.

In Provence an egg is given to a newborn child, along with bread, salt, and a knitting needle. This is to ensure that the child will be whole as an egg (that is, have all his faculties), good as bread, sharp as salt, and straight as a needle. Interestingly enough, red hard-boiled eggs are presented with congratulations on the birth of a child in China and among Chinese people in many parts of the world.

An African tribe which was once Christian, as all northern Africa was at one time, and is now entirely Muslim has a custom of coloring eggs.

According to an entry in an expense book, Edward I of England in 1290 purchased 450 eggs to be colored or covered with gold leaf. The eggs were given to members of the royal household. Henry VIII received a Paschal egg in a silver filigree case from the Vatican one year.

Among Near East Christians the custom of exchanging eggs goes back so far no one remembers how it started. The eggs are colored red to represent the blood of Christ. In Armenia the eggs were blown out and the empty shells had pictures of the risen Christ, the Virgin Mary, and other religious insignia. Russians painted eggs with patterns and greetings: "Christ is risen," or something like "Eat and think of me." Polish eggs had fish, crosses, and other religious symbols. There it used to be the custom for girls to give especially attractive eggs wrapped in an embroidered scarf or kerchief to their favorite admirers. If the men cared to, they reciprocated with gifts of clothing.

Probably the height of the art of coloring eggs was reached by the Ukrainians with their *pysanki*. Many of these beautiful eggs were kept for generations as heirlooms. A design of melted beeswax was applied with a stylus. The egg was then dipped in a succession of dye baths. After each dipping, wax was painted over the area where the preceding color was to remain—it was much the same process as the batiks made by women in Indonesia. The egg designs were original and no attempt was made to have any two alike. During the long Lenten evenings the girls and women worked at this. The eggs were dried out in the oven so that eventually nothing was left but the shell with its delicate decoration.

The Pennsylvania Dutch decorated eggs with scratch carving. First the eggs were dyed an attractive color, then a design was scratched into the shell with a sharp knife or other pointed tool. Designs included the usual tulips, *distelfinks*, flat hearts, butterflies, and elephants. Some of these eggs have lasted over a hundred years. Scratch carving on eggs was popular in Switzerland in the 1880's and was also done in Germany.

Dyes in rural areas were often made from native materials. Onion skins were used; alder catkins and hickory bark made yellow dye, madder root made light red, and coffee and walnut shells were used for brown. Sometimes patterns from calico were transferred onto the eggs. A woolly pith from a swamp rush has been used for egg decorating, and in Austria they wrapped the eggs in ferns and leaves before boiling so the pattern would be left on the eggs.

In Balkan countries it was believed that painted eggs could protect a house from evil, and planted in the ground they protected the vines. Many superstitions have surrounded eggs laid on Good Friday. Pennsylvania Dutch farmers would not sell these eggs, but kept them because they could cure ailments. Others thought they were good to extinguish fires. It was a good omen to eat an egg laid on Good Friday on the same day, but they were believed to keep fresh indefinitely.

There is a lovely story from the German writer, Christoph von Schmid, which tells of a beautiful titled woman who suddenly appeared in a mountain village with her children and one servant. Because of her kindnesses the people came to love her, although she remained a mystery to them. At Easter she gave a party for the children of the village and presented each with a colored egg on which she had written a motto. One of these eggs finally reached her husband, who had been searching everywhere for her to take her home to their castle that he had finally regained from a villainous knight. The custom of coloring eggs is supposed to have started from this.

Another story, by Carolyn Sherwin Bailey, tells of the origin of the hollow sugar egg, with a scene inside. The egg was presented in a competition for a new and different Easter egg to amuse the young prince and princess. Elaborate carved, jeweled, and huge toy eggs were submitted,

but the prize went to the little old lady in the apron who knew what would delight children.

These have become part of the folklore of the Easter egg, considered by some to be a pagan symbol, by others a legitimate representation of resurrection. Whether we like it or not, the egg is very much a part of the celebration of Easter. Even people who don't particularly enjoy eating hard-boiled eggs will have one for Easter breakfast when it is beautifully colored.

New clothes, beautiful flowers from unsightly bulbs, baby chicks, colored eggs, sunrise—all speak of beginnings. And every time Easter arrives, it is a new beginning. We look back on the resurrection of Christ as a turning point of history, but for us each Easter is a new opportunity for beginning again. And this is why the holiday never loses its appeal.

In a very real way each new day gives us a new start. St. Francis is supposed to have repeated each morning, "Today I begin again to be Christian." Dwight L. Moody said, "Every day I have a little new birth." Sarah Chauncey Woolsey, writing under her pen name of Susan Coolidge, put this thought very beautifully in her poem:

Begin Again

Every day is a fresh beginning,
  Every morn is the world made new,
You who are weary of sorrow and sinning,
  Here is a beautiful hope for you,—
A hope for me and a hope for you.

Every day is a fresh beginning;
  Listen, my soul, to the glad refrain,
And, spite of old sorrow and older sinning,
  And puzzles forecasted and possible pain,
Take heart with the day, and begin again.

5. *The Joy of Celebration*

THE word "celebration" is used more in churches today than formerly. Those with a Puritan heritage have thought only of the merrymaking aspect. Liturgical churches have long related it to solemn rites and ceremonies. Celebration means both. Much of the Sunday morning worship service is celebration but so also is much that goes on in small groups, in vacation church school, youth outings, coffee hours.

Perhaps the best place for celebration of Christian faith

is in the home. What a happy word "family" is! It envisions loving parents caring for joyful children. Some of us have warm memories of our families, while others think of them as something from which they want to get away. A family has great capacity for giving joy to its members—and also for providing suffering. Paul speaks in Ephesians of "the Father . . . of whom the whole family in heaven and earth is named." And for those who are feeling left out, "God setteth the solitary in families." Apparently the family is a planned unit of human society—it didn't just happen. Nobody has been able to improve upon it as a means of nurturing the young in today's complex world, though some primitive peoples have succeeded in communal forms of living.

In our day terrific pressures are put on the family. There are so many places for each family member to be, so much to be done, the problems of transporting each one to his next appointment. The father has unusual stresses because of business, and the mother is torn between her desire to make a meaningful contribution to life and the need to be chauffeur, cook, housemaid, laundress, and homework-tutor. There is little time when they are all together and even less time when they are relaxed together. Happy is the family that meets at the point of religious experience.

Some religious experience happens far from church. Fortunate the parent who is able to encourage and observe a child's sense of wonder about a cobweb or a crocus and to answer the first tentative questions about the meaning of the universe and life.

How do you teach your child the meaning of Easter? Will he get it from the basket of colored eggs with fluffy chicks and a chocolate rabbit? Will he absorb it by dressing up in new clothes and sitting through an adult service on Easter morning and observing the crowded sanctuary and beautiful lilies? He may, but the experience will have more meaning for him if he has been patiently prepared by experience with things he can see and feel and taste during the days and weeks before.

"What does Easter mean?" a child may ask. Immediately you launch into the significance of the Resurrection of Jesus and its implications of immortality for all of us.

"But what does the *word* 'Easter' mean?" the child persists. Ah, there you have a question. Generations have been raised on the theory that the word "Easter" came from pagan mythology. The Venerable Bede, an English historian and theologian of the eighth century, when the holiday first began to be called Easter, wrote that it was named for Eostre, an Anglo-Saxon goddess. This must have been conjecture on his part, because recent scholars can locate no reference to such a goddess in northern mythology.

The German word *Ostern*, as well as its English equivalent, "Easter," is derived from the Norse *eostur, eastur,* or *ostara,* which meant "the season of the growing sun," "the season of new birth." A similar word, *ost* or "east," is used for the direction in which the sun rises. So it looks as if our English word for the spring holiday commemorating the Resurrection comes from the season and not a pagan deity. There is plenty of symbolism in the sun if you are looking for it—Sun of Righteousness, the Light that lighteth all men, Sun of my Soul, Thou Saviour Dear.

Some interesting historic events have been connected with Easter. A child's geography book is affected by this date. Easter Island comes immediately to mind, an island in the South Pacific discovered over fifty years before America became a nation, by a Dutch explorer named Roggeveen. Fortunately for students, he didn't name it for himself but for the day on which he landed—Easter Day, 1722. The natives of the lonely little island call it Frontier of Heaven.

An earlier Easter discovery is closer to us—Ponce de Leon first sighted the land he named Florida on Easter morning, March 27, 1513. The Spanish expression *Pascua Florida* was originally the term for Palm Sunday and was later applied to all of Holy Week, and from it the Flamingo state got its name.

Many foods are connected by tradition with the period of Lent and the festival of Easter. By reviving an ancient custom we can feel a kinship with the past and perhaps understand a little better the people who lived in those times and appreciate what we have today.

Pretzels were once a special Lenten food, particularly in Austria, Germany, and Poland. The word *Brezel* probably comes from *brachiatus*, having branchlike arms. The shape of the pretzel reminded someone of arms folded in prayer. They were first made in the fifth century at the Vatican and later were distributed to poor people on certain days of Lent. From Wednesday through Saturday of Holy Week this was the only bread eaten in some places, probably because it was unleavened, made only of flour, salt, and water. In Austria, pretzels could be purchased from a vendor called a *Brezelmann*, and were hung on palm branches as part of the celebration of Palm Sunday. Only in the last century have they been available all year round.

Many people know that pancakes are eaten on Shrove Tuesday without knowing exactly why. Since the fats and eggs had to be used up before the strict fast, these were put into rich pancakes—often the last fried food until Easter. In Liberty, Kansas, on Shrove Tuesday, a group of women run a race, each carrying a skillet with a pancake,

and the results are usually announced nationwide on the evening newscast. The origin of this unusual race goes back to a housewife in Olney, England, in the year 1445. The people depended on the church bell to indicate that it was time to go to the church for confession on Shrove Tuesday. This particular housewife was a little late with her work that day, and the bell caught her just as she was making herself some pancakes for lunch. She knew she would have a long wait at the church and needed the food but hesitated to be late, so she hurried off to church carrying the pancake on the griddle. The spectacle of the woman running through the town carrying the griddle so amused the populace that a pancake race grew out of the incident, but it was abandoned before many years had passed.

In 1950 the five-hundred-year-old race was revived across the Atlantic in the town of Liberal, Kansas, where a group of churchwomen ran a 415-yard course from the town pump to the church. This was exploited by the Chamber of Commerce with the result that a challenge was issued to the housewives of Olney, England. So now on Pancake Tuesday women in both towns run courses of the same distance and results are compared by telephone. Of course with typical American promotional expertise, Pancake Day in Liberal (pop., 1960, 13,813) has become a profitable three-day affair, attracting visitors from a great distance, to say nothing of television cameramen.

Fastnachtskuchen is a doughnut, usually cut square without a hole, made by Germans and our Pennsylvania Dutch to eat on Shrove Tuesday. Sometimes a raised doughnut will go by this name but the true *Fastnachtskuchen* (Night of the Fast cake) has no yeast but is made with sour cream, soda, sugar, and egg. It is eaten only on this day, split and spread with quince or crabapple jelly. Norway has a special lenten roll called *fastelavnsboller*. Filled with whipped cream and rolled in sugar, it is a gourmet delight. In Sweden the bun is split, spread with marzipan, topped with whipped cream and served with hot milk.

Palm Sunday has a number of foods connected with it. Fig Sunday is another name for the day in some places, where figs or fig pudding were served at the midday meal while someone told or read the story of the barren fig tree. A certain type of Italian fig when cut through shows a green cross against white pulp and is highly prized at this

time. Devout Canary Islanders always cut bananas length-
wise, for they show a cross when cut across.

In Wales the day is called Carling Sunday. On that day
people eat carlings, gray peas that are soaked in water, then
fried in butter. Small cakes stamped with the Agnus Dei
(lamb and banner) are given to each parishioner as he leaves
the service that morning.

Maundy Thursday is called Green Thursday in much of
the world, and it is customary to eat green vegetables and
herbs on that day. A favorite dish among German Protestants is kale cooked with pork and onions. In Czechoslovakia breakfast cakes of dough twisted to look like rope
are called Judases and eaten with honey on this day. The
Easter lamb cake, made in a hinged or two-part mold
to form the shape of a lamb lying down, is traditionally
baked on Thursday. The custom, which comes to us from
Europe—in Czechoslovakia the cake is called *beranek*—is
growing in importance here. Usually the lamb is frosted
and covered with coconut to simulate wool.

Good Friday is noted for hot cross buns, though in
America they are served throughout the Lenten period.
These yeast buns made with currants or raisins wear a white
cross in frosting on top. Actually, this may have a pre-
Christian origin, since it is known that cross-marked rolls
were used in the worship of Diana. Certainly the signifi-
cance of the cross was not the same for the Greeks and
Romans as for Christians.

In Chelsea, England, there were two royal bun houses
which sold the buns in the piazza in front of the shop from
6 A.M. to 6 P.M. that day. Eating hot cross buns was supposed to provide a charm against bad luck, particularly

fire. Their special powers also included keeping rats out of the corn and preventing shipwreck. The buns are said to have originated in 1361 at St. Alban's Abbey when a monk baked them to give to the poor. Rich with currants, raisins, and citron, they must have seemed a magnificent bounty. Of course other people decided that they shouldn't waste something so good on the poor, and before long everybody was eating hot cross buns on Good Friday, often buying them from street vendors who started out early in the morning. Everybody is familiar with the vendor's cry, "One a penny, two a penny, hot cross buns!"

There are many special Easter breads prepared to eat on Easter. The Russian *paska*, made with flour, cottage cheese, sugar, raisins, eggs, and milk, is baked in a mold to make a firm square cake about eight inches high with a cross on each side. Small cakes, each with a taper, were taken to church to be blessed at the midnight service.

In Germany and Austria an Easter yeast bread with raisins called *Osterstollen* is made in long loaves of twisted or braided strands. *Butterkuchen* is a flat yeast bread dotted with butter, cinnamon, and sugar. Another Austrian Easter bread, *Osterlaib*, is a large flat round leaf marked with a cross or a lamb. *Bábovka* is a coffee bread from Czechoslovakia, baked in a round fluted cake form with a hole in the middle. This name is also applied to the pound-cake type. A similar Polish coffee cake is called *baba* and includes nuts and fruit. The fluted pan is supposed to resemble a woman's skirt. *Mazanec* is another Czech rich coffeecake, similar to the Russian *kulich* which is baked in cylinder shape. The Greek Easter bread is always decorated with blanched almonds. Moravians brought to this country their old-world recipe for sugar cake which is served in the church after the early dawn service. Poland has a very sweet Easter pastry called *mazurki*, made with honey and filled with nuts and fruits. Syrian and Jordanian Christians celebrate with special honey pastries of the *baklava* type. In some parts of Ireland the traditional Easter breakfast is "golden bread," similar to French toast.

In America ham is traditional for Easter dinner. The custom was introduced by William the Conqueror. He also had *gammon* (unsliced bacon), red herrings, corn, salad, and tansy pudding. The latter was flavored with the leaves of a rather bitter-tasting aromatic weed. It has been suggested that pork was traditional because the pig is a symbol of good luck and prosperity in many lands. The German expression *Schwein haben* means "good luck"—literally, "to have a pig." Perhaps the prosperity connotation is borne out by the popularity of piggy banks. In Transylvania the ham is baked in a covering of bread dough. Hungarians are known for their Easter meat loaf of chopped pork, ham, eggs, bread, and spices.

From the ninth century on through many centuries the Pope always had roast lamb for Easter dinner. Lamb is still the favored Easter food in many parts of Eastern Europe. If lamb is not served, frequently figures of a lamb made of butter, pastry, or sugar are used as table centerpieces at this season.

The Italians have a traditional dessert dating from medieval times called Easter Pie which is more of a cheese cake, though more substantial than our American version. It has a tender cooky-type crust called *pasta frolla*. In this country children enjoy cookies in the shapes of chicks and bunnies, cakes in the shape of an egg or Easter hat. Baking cookies is a project the youngsters should certainly share.

Children may enjoy making edible Easter baskets to hold candy eggs. This can easily be done by melting a half pound of marshmallows with a third of a cup of butter or

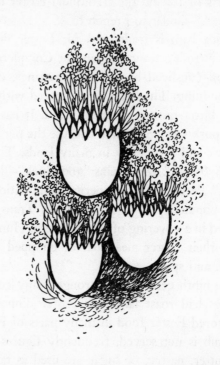

margarine over hot water and pouring this over a package of crisp rice cereal (shredded biscuits or puffed) in a bowl. When evenly coated, cool for a few minutes, then fill buttered cereal bowls three quarters full and twist a glass or cup which has been buttered on the outside in the sticky mixture to shape a nest. Remove the glass and the next day loosen the "rice basket" from the bowl with a small knife. Then fill it with jelly beans.

A planting project will heighten a child's anticipation of Easter. Save a number of eggshell halves. Fill them with soil and set them in egg cups or supports cut from an egg carton. Moisten the soil with a spoonful of water and plant a marigold, petunia, or grapefruit seed in it. For faster results, sprinkle grass seed over the soil. Place in a sunny window and watch for shoots.

A more complicated project that will have great interest for older children is an egg tree. There has been increased interest in this in recent years in America, partly due to a popular children's book titled *The Egg Tree* by Katherine Milhous. Hanging colored eggs on an evergreen or bare tree branch in the house is a Pennsylvania Dutch custom which began nearly a century ago. The custom obviously came from Germany, though it is found in other northern countries, too. Children saved colored bird eggs, which made an interesting sight together with dyed or painted hen, duck, or turkey eggs. Sometimes natural colored eggs were hung on bushes or small trees outdoors.

The eggs, of course, are hollow shells. To keep the shell whole, prick both ends of the egg with a needle or pin and carefully blow the contents out into a dish. The hole at one end will need to be a little larger than at the blowing end. Rinse the shell with water, blowing this out, too. Dye or paint in any color desired and attach a loop of colored ribbon with glue. Hang on a tree branch, small end down.

For a variation, colored half-shells in which you have glued tiny artificial flowers or cottony chicks or tiny can-

dies can be hung by ribbons. Or the whole eggshells may
be impaled on the spines of a thorn branch or yucca plant.

In my childhood the preparing of baskets to receive the
eggs was the responsibility of us children. Occasionally new
baskets were bought or some were left over from the year
before, but usually we made our own from cardboard
boxes and crepe paper. One year I decided to grow a basket.
Several weeks before Easter I planted grass seed in a baking pan and tended it carefully. By Easter the grass was
about two inches high, providing a very good nest for
the colored eggs.

Egg coloring certainly should be an activity in which
children share as soon as they are able to dip an egg in
dye. As they grow older, coloring eggs may give opportunity for developing real artistic talent.

Both seeds and eggs are symbols of new life and represent a form of resurrection. Children can learn the wonder
of life and growing things long before they can understand the theological implications of Easter.

The origin of egg rolling is rather difficult to determine.
The custom has long been popular in Europe and America.
In Washington, D. C., children have been doing it on the
White House lawn or at the Capitol since the days of
James Madison. There are variations, but usually each
child brings his own eggs and finds his own competition,
and the one whose egg rolls the farthest without getting
cracked is the winner. In New York City's Central Park
a more formal egg rolling contest has been conducted since
World War II with contestants using wooden eggs and
wooden spoons, and with prizes awarded. Competition is
limited to children aged five to twelve.

In the eighteenth century egg races were an important part of the Easter festival in some parts of France, and a hogshead of cider was given as prize.

An old tale has it that in the time of the Crusades egg rolling was a test for fitness of young knights, but it seems a rather pallid test for such violent times. I prefer the theory that egg rolling comes from the custom in Greenwich, England, of people going to a hill outside town on Easter and rolling down the grassy slope. This was a people rolling, not egg rolling, and it is an activity most children—and some adults—still delight in.

Hunting eggs that have been hidden is an activity many children enjoy. Some families hide notes with clues which send the children on a hunt that ends with the Easter baskets.

One of the sidelights of Easter that can help children expand their horizons is the sale of Easter seals to help crippled children. The idea of raising money through an Easter seal, of course, came from the success of the Christmas seal, originated by Danish postal clerk Elmer Holboll in 1903. In 1934, at the height of the Depression, the Easter seal was adopted as a means of raising funds to help crippled children. "Easter means Resurrection and New Life; and the rehabilitation of crippled children means... new life and activity...physically, mentally, and spiritually," said Paul H. King, then president of the sponsoring society. Around three million dollars has been raised from the seals annually, helping thousands of children to gain a new opportunity for life.

Though Easter has never become as much a gift-giving time as Christmas, there has been some emphasis given to this idea, particularly by department stores. Small children are usually given stuffed animals, older ones may receive games or sporting equipment. But how much better to stress this as a time to think of others! This might be a good time to give toys to less privileged children, to prepare homemade gifts for grandparents, or take eggs or candy to lonely elderly neighbors. Since most children receive new clothes for Easter, they could share in preparing and packing their outgrown clothes to send to children who could wear them, perhaps in another country. As adults find a unity in the thought of Lent and Easter kept by Christians all over the world, children also can learn the joy of being a part of a worldwide family.

Sometimes a child makes a special commitment at Eastertime by being baptized or confirmed. It is something the young person does on his own, yet it is a time when the support and happiness of his family becomes especially meaningful.

Lent is intended to be a time of meditating on the meaning of the Christian life, a time to bring our lives into closer communion with God. It is to be hoped that this also brings us closer to those with whom we are in intimate daily contact. As we learn from the Master who washed His disciples' feet, may we put into practice "by love serve one another" (Galatians 5:13) in our homes.

Perhaps a good project for the family would be the selection of Scripture verses with particular pertinence to home life to be put on the kitchen bulletin board or read at the breakfast table. They would include such practical advice as "Be courteous" (I Peter 3:8) "Be ye kind one to another, tender-hearted, forgiving one another" (Ephesians 4:32); "Let us not be weary in well-doing" (Galatians 6:9); "Love is never boastful, nor conceited, nor rude" (I Corinthians 13:5, New English Bible). Some families like to keep a little bank or mite box on the table during Lent and place money in it each day to send to people who are needy. Children can learn the joy of sharing if one meal a week is particularly simple and inexpensive so the cost of a usual meal may be put in the box. It is possible to secure samples of multipurpose food (MPF) from Meals for Millions, Los Angeles, to make the point even clearer.

Easter is a time to express our joy in family life, to thank God, and to pray for families everywhere—and to invite a lonely person to share our Easter dinner.

Here are several prayers which may have meaning for families:

Be present with us, O Lord, in our daily duties, and grant to those who dwell in this house the strength and protection of Thy continual help; that Thou mayest be known as the Master of the family and the defender of this home; through Jesus Christ our Lord.

—Gelasian Sacramentary

Heavenly Father, after whom all fatherhood in heaven and earth is named: Bless, we beseech Thee, all children, and give to their parents and to all in whose charge they may be, the spirit of wisdom and love: so that the home in which they grow up may be to them an image of Thy Kingdom, and the care of their parents a likeness of Thy love; through Jesus Christ our Lord.

—Prayers of the World-Wide Church

O Christ our Lord, who didst go forth in homelessness that Thou mightest find a home in every man and that every man might find a home in Thee: we bring before Thee at this time all thy homeless ones, all who are in exile or in suffering, all refugees; grant them the sense of being held fast in Thee, and enable all who love Thee to strive together for a world which shall be closer to Thy kingdom, in which men may live together as a family, each caring for all, and all caring for each, for the sake of peace.

—GEORGE APPLETON

Lord God Almighty, Father of every family, against whom no door can be shut: Enter all homes, we beseech Thee, with the angel of Thy presence, to hallow them in pureness and beauty of love; and by Thy dear Son, born in a stable, move our hearts to hear the cry of the homeless, and to convert all sordid and bitter dwellings into households of Thine; through Jesus Christ our Lord.

—E. MILNER-WHITE

In some homes the practice of regular family worship has grown out of a Lenten discipline of devotions together at the table. Whether worship or religious instruction in the home are regular or spontaneous, they are important factors in the children's spiritual development. And sometimes quite spiritual conversations have arisen from the explanations given in response to questions about food or customs. In small ways seeds of faith are planted and nurtured.

Holidays are for celebrating. It takes extra effort, of course. And it takes imagination to do it well. But the rewards in meaningful experience, in shared happiness, in memories to last a lifetime are well worth all that is expended. Children should not miss the joy of celebration.

6. *The Joy of Communication*

ONE of life's greatest joys is that of creating. Success in making a thing of beauty or usefulness is the joy of the craftsman. Baking a cake, growing a prize dahlia, building a book shelf, writing a short story, playing a sonata, raising a family, erecting a church, completing a finger painting, all have something in common.

Many of us do creative work for the satisfaction we gain from it personally. Some are privileged to create for others in the realms of music, art, dramatics, philosophy, literature, handicrafts. When others grasp the thought behind what we create, we are communicating, and this carries its own joy.

There is joy on the part of the recipient, too. There cannot be a communicator without one communicated to. For most of us, enjoyment of the arts means being on the receiving end of the communication. We see a play or a movie and come out with a new thought or a sense of pleasure or a happy tune running through our heads. We read a book which sets us thinking in a whole new vein or puts into words an idea that we have held in an unformed fashion, and we can hardly wait to tell someone else who will understand about the exciting thoughts which have been communicated to us.

We visit an art museum or study reproductions of great paintings, trying to expose ourselves to greatness, hoping to understand what is being said to us by the painter. We go through historic old houses that have been restored, with furnishings of the period, seeking to learn from the people who lived there long ago some wisdom that will be useful to us today. We go to church and wait for the silence, the light filtering through the stained glass, the surging organ, the words of the minister, or the mystery of the sacrament to communicate God's message to us.

The Passion of Christ is probably the subject which has been more often portrayed by artists than any other, at least in the Western world. Even a person with a good knowledge of classical painters and sculptors is overwhelmed with the great number of unknown artists who carved altar pieces or painted icons or murals showing some scene from Jesus' last week.

Probably the best-known religious painting in the world is Leonardo da Vinci's "Last Supper." And it must be the most copied. So many wood carvings have been made from it that sometimes people forget that the original was painted right on a church wall. Usually the prints one sees look better than the actual painting at the Santa Maria della Gracie Church in Milan, which is cracked and faded. The influence of Leonardo's arrangement of figures has persisted in many later representations, though the knots have been removed from the corners of the table cloth. A recent rather happy and quite Jewish-looking setting for this event can be seen in the Jambor painting with the same title.

One of the better-known paintings is Warner E. Sallman's "Christ in Gethsemane" because of the many reproductions distributed around the country. This has replaced in many cases the well-known Hofmann painting of the scene and is quite similar in position. The original of the Hofmann hangs in a tiny chapel off the vestibule of New York City's Riverside Church. While these paintings are often not considered in the same light as the great masterpieces of the ages, they have served a devotional purpose and have provided inspiration to many persons. One painting of this scene shows Christ in agony in a prone position, rather than kneeling at a stone.

There are a number of paintings of the betrayal and arrest, showing Judas stepping into the light while the soldiers with torches hover in the dark background of the picture. In the National Gallery hangs an El Greco portrayal of the cleansing of the temple called "Christ Driving the Traders from the Temple." It has beautiful colors and some motion but a rather placid Christ. We have all seen pictures of the trial before Pilate and of Peter's denial. There is a haunting quality about Peter's remorse in Harroch's painting of the scene, just as Peter notices that the cock has crowed and Jesus turns to look at him.

While there are thousands of representations of the Crucifixion, some of the modern artists have been getting recognition for their work on this subject. And some of these speak very expressively to people today. The clean, cold lines of Salvador Dali's "Crucifixion" in the Metropolitan Museum of Art accentuate the aloneness of the event, while other representations such as the George Guazava in the Soho Gallery, the Jan Styka at Forest Lawn Chapel, and the J. Ensor in Brussels emphasize the crowd and confusion. Dali's better-known crucifixion scene, titled "Christ of St. John of the Cross," in the Glasgow Art Gallery was originally planned as a ceiling piece for a church, which may account for the unusual perspective, though to many viewers this seems to represent the event from God's viewpoint rather than man's.

The Munkacsy "Christ on Calvary," as well as "Christ Before Pilate," is owned by the John Wanamaker family and is displayed in the Philadelphia store every year during Holy Week. Suffering is very clearly expressed in Georges Rouault's "Christ Mocked by Soldiers" in the Museum of Modern Art, New York. Though it has an almost stained-glass effect and the soldiers look like clowns, this is a picture which communicates emotion to young people.

Probably everyone knows about Michelangelo's "Pietà" since it has been at the World's Fair in New York. This is one of the great artist's earlier works, executed when he was nineteen. Americans considered it a great privilege to have had the masterpiece for two years, though large sums of money had to be spent to get it here and to keep the

marble from cracking in the humid New York climate.
In European museums one finds many Pietàs executed in
wood, stone, plaster, and other media, but probably no
sculpture of Mary and the dead Christ surpasses that by the
fifteenth-century Michelangelo. The book and motion picture, *The Agony and the Ecstasy,* have focused further
attention on this great work. There are also famous paintings of Jesus in death. Rubens' "Descent from the Cross"
is a well-known example.

We can remember paintings from our early religious
training showing the disciples Peter and John hurrying to
the tomb, Christ appearing to Mary Magdalene, to the
gathered disciples, and eating with the two in Emmaus.
Rembrandt van Rijn, the devout Dutch painter of the sev-
enteenth century, has a very serene portrayal of the latter.
"The Supper at Emmaus" by German Rudolf Eichstädt
is more modern and shows Jesus beginning to disappear.

An often-told story about a picture relates the experience
of the young Count von Zinzendorf who was so moved
by a painting showing Christ wearing a crown of thorns
with the caption, "This have I done for thee. What hast
thou done for me?" that he devoted his life and fortune to
Christ. He is noted for his great support of and leadership
in the Moravian movement.

A quite different type of artist concerned with the Easter
season was Carl Fabergé, a goldsmith and jeweler of the
late nineteenth and early twentieth centuries who created
art objects in the shape of eggs which are still most sought-
after, forty-five years after his death. In 1961 an exhibit of
Easter eggs and other priceless objects by Fabergé was held
at the Corcoran Art Gallery in Washington, D.C.

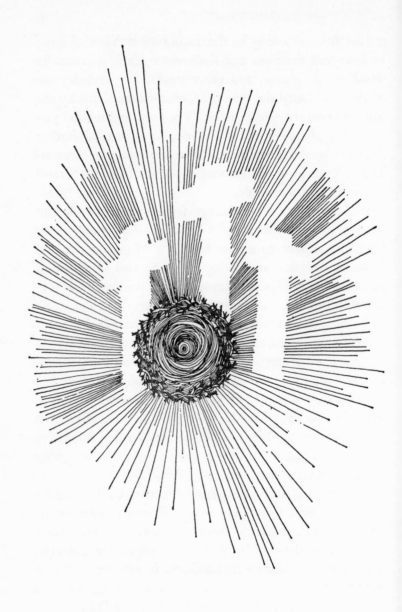

Carl Fabergé came from a family of French Huguenots who moved to Russia to escape persecution. There he became famous for imaginative designs in jewelry, both to wear and to look at. The Czar became one of his chief patrons, and he created many Easter eggs containing ingenious surprises which were to be presents for the Czarina. The English Prince Consort Albert and most of the royalty of Europe bought his whimsical and beautiful objects. His work grew so that he had to train a corps of assistants, but the master inspected every piece and if it failed to meet his rigid standards, it was scrapped. The workshop closed with the war in 1914 and Fabergé left the country. The great artist and craftsman died in Lausanne, Switzerland, in 1920, but the Fabergé eggs are valued as highly as ever today.

A number of great and familiar pieces of music are connected with the Easter season. The opera *Parsifal*, by Richard Wagner, is usually performed on or near Good Friday, because it is concerned with the story of the Holy Grail. The knights of the Grail were supposed to be soldiers assigned to the task of protecting the cup which had held the blood of the crucified Christ. *Lohengrin* is also related to this theme, but Wagner considered *Parsifal* "a consecrational festival play," not just theatrical entertainment. Its theme is the spiritual redemption of man through the sacrifice of a Saviour, and the music begins with the theme of the Eucharist. The "Dresden Amen," sung in many churches, appears early in the opera.

"Stabat Mater Dolorosa" (Stands the Sorrowing Mother) originally was written as a prayer for private devotion by an unknown author in the thirteenth century. The Latin words have been translated into the vernacular in all Christian nations. It is sung to a number of tunes, including a German hymn that comes from a 1661 hymnbook. Palestrina wrote a beautiful cantata in the sixteenth century, as did the young Pergolesi early in the eighteenth. Rossini's later one is rather operatic and a favorite showpiece of tenors and sopranos. Dvořák's "Stabat Mater," first presented in London in 1884, is somewhat more substantial than Rossini's.

The hymn "O Sacred Head Now Wounded" by Paul Gerhardt, set to the tune of an old German song composed by Hans L. Hassler and published in 1601, is sung in both Protestant and Catholic churches. The melody is used by Bach in his *St. Matthew Passion*. The Bach Passions are among the most often-heard music at this time of year.

Allegri's *Miserere*, part of Tenebrae (the matins and lauds sung on Wednesday, Thursday, and Friday of Holy Week), was at one time used only in the Sistine Chapel and the Pope did not allow it to be published. The young Mozart, aged fourteen at the time, attended with his father and was fascinated by the music; he went home and wrote it out from memory and sent it to the organist for correction. Only two or three notes differed from the manuscript used at the Chapel. The Pope was so impressed with the boy's feat that he gave permission for its publication.

Mozart is not the only composer who demonstrated an interest in religious music at an early age. Handel wrote a Passion at the age of nineteen, though it is overshadowed by his later *Messiah*. Beethoven's oratorio, *Christ on the Mount of Olives*, was written at the age of thirty. It was criticized as theatrical and many thought he should not have had a character representing Jesus. The music is majestic, particularly the often sung "Hallelujah Chorus."

The words of Christ from the Cross have fascinated musicians. Franz Joseph Haydn composed a *Seven Last Words* oratorio for the Three Hours' Devotion of the Cathedral of Cádiz, Spain. There is a lovely one by Heinrich Schütz, and Gounod's is often performed today in both Catholic and Protestant churches. A *Seven Last Words* by another Frenchman, Théodore Dubois, which was first performed in Paris in 1869, has long been a favorite here.

César Franck's *Redemption* and Maunder's *Olivet to Calvary*, once very popular, are not done as often now. Gaul's *Holy City* was a favorite in some areas. "Unfold, Ye Portals" is all we ever hear of Gounod's *Redemption* today. But Sir John Stainer's majestic *Crucifixion* never seems to lose its appeal. The Easter section of Handel's *Messiah* is often sung, of course.

On Good Friday one of several Requiems may be sung. The Fauré is generally liked better than the Brahms. A new one by Maurice Duruflé is gaining interest. New music is being written for the season, an example being Alan Hovhaness' *Easter Cantata* written for the Columbia Broadcasting Company and first performed in Boston in 1955. But most churchgoers prefer the old music.

For many, it would not be Palm Sunday without hearing the anthem "The Palms" by Jean Baptiste Fauré (not to be confused with Gabriel Urbain Fauré, who wrote the *Requiem*), a French operatic baritone who died in 1914. He wrote several vocal pieces but only this one remains. Another Palm Sunday anthem we used to hear a great deal is "Open the Gates of the Temple" by Knapp, incorporating a section of Handel's "I Know That My Redeemer Liveth."

The most famous instrumental music of the season is the *Russian Easter Overture* by Nikolai A. Rimski-Korsakov, a Russian composer who died in 1908. The music is based on canticles of the Orthodox Church.

Though it is not related at all to the resurrection of Christ, Gustav Mahler's *Resurrection Symphony* is sometimes played at this time of year. In this symphony he was contemplating death and resurrection for man as a prelude to a new and purified life.

Most of the congregational hymns that we use in church during Holy Week date from the middle of the nineteenth century. Several relate to the agony in Gethsemane and are quite descriptive. " 'Tis Midnight and on Olive's Brow the Star Is Dimmed That Lately Shone" was written by William B. Tappan, an American, in 1822. "Go to dark Gethsemane, ye that feel the tempter's power; your Redeemer's conflict see; watch with Him one bitter hour" by James Montgomery (1820), is often sung at a three-hour Good Friday service. The tune "Gethsemane" by Richard Redhead was first used with the words in 1853. In the same somber mood, "In the Hour of Trial" is a later hymn by Montgomery. Just as poignant, though less theological, is "Into the Woods My Master Went, Clean Forspent, Forspent" by Sidney Lanier, a poet and English professor at Johns Hopkins University. The poem became a hymn with the addition of Peter Lutkin's music in 1904.

Our favorite hymns about the Cross or the Crucifixion are mostly British. "In the Cross of Christ I Glory" is by Sir

John Bowring, who was a Member of Parliament and governor of Hong Kong. The wall of the ruined church, topped by the cross, which inspired this hymn still stands today in Macao as a memorial to Robert Morrison and the other early missionaries to China. "Beneath the Cross of Jesus" was written by a Scottish woman, Elizabeth Clephane, a year before her death at the age of thirty-nine. The tune "St. Christopher," to which this is sung, was composed by Frederick Charles Maker, a lifetime resident of Bristol, England.

"There Is a Green Hill Far Away" seems to be exclusively a Lenten hymn, though it is certainly suitable at any time. Written for a sick child by an Irishwoman, Cecil Frances Alexander, it has been universally loved by adults. Its most familiar musical setting is that of George C. Stebbins, added in 1878, thirty years after the poem was written.

Often called the greatest hymn in the English language, Isaac Watts' "When I Survey the Wondrous Cross" is universally loved and has stood the test of time, for it was written in 1707. It is sung to at least three lovely tunes, one of which is "Hamburg," from a sixth century Gregorian chant.

When Americans have been polled on their favorite hymn, it has usually turned out to be George Bennard's "The Old Rugged Cross." This is a newcomer to the field, copyrighted in 1913, and one of the few popular hymns written by an American. Hymnologists are always amused when people say they prefer the old hymns and come up with this quite recent one as an example. It has been called poor music and inferior poetry, but it has spoken to thousands. In many ways the rough cross, signifying suffering

and shame, takes one a little closer to the actual Crucifixion
scene than the symbol we have made of the cross "towering
o'er the wrecks of time." Of course both concepts are valid.

Several Negro spirituals bring out the poignance of the
Crucifixion, which a suffering people could well understand. "He Never Said a Mumblin' Word" tells the whole
story: "See how they done my Lord, led Him into Pilate's
hall, put on Him a thorny crown, put on Him a purple
robe, nailed Him to the cross. He suffered on the cross;
they pierced Him in the side; He bowed His head and
died"; and after each line comes the refrain, "An' He
never said a mumblin' word." Another touching spiritual,
used more and more as a hymn, is "Were You There When
They Crucified My Lord?" The traditional melody was
arranged by Charles Winfred Douglas and first published
in 1899. The well-known Negro tenor Roland Hayes is
credited with making it famous.

Christina Rossetti's "The Tempest Over and Gone" is
one of the few hymns for Holy Saturday. It has a mood
of quiet waiting: "The Strong Man sleeps; all stars keep
vigil watching for the Sun; the moon her vigil keeps."

Easter hymns were written as early as the second century. We sing one today by John of Damascus which is
believed to date from the eighth century. It begins, "The
day of resurrection—Earth, tell it out abroad; the passover
of gladness, the passover of God." It was translated into
English by John Mason Neale in 1862. Dr. Neale is known
for Easter hymns of his own, particularly "The World Itself Keeps Easter Day and Easter Larks Are Singing." It
has more than birds and flowers, however, telling in suc-
ceeding stanzas the story of the three Marys at the tomb

on Easter morning, the angel's message, and Jesus' appearance to Magdalene. The conclusion is "The Lord of all things lives anew, and all His works are living too. Alleluia!"

"Alleluia" seems to be the most popular word in Easter hymns. Originally it was used only at Easter but eventually spread through the liturgy. It became a popular chant for workers, particularly for boatmen while they were rowing. For most of us it would not be Easter without Charles Wesley's hymn, "Christ the Lord Is Risen Today," which has an "alleluia" after each line in the four stanzas. Written in 1739, this hymn is usually sung to a 1798 tune composed by J. Worgan.

A newer hymn that seems to be essential on Easter and is sung only that one day is "Christ Arose" by Robert Lowry, copyrighted in 1916. Since Lowry wrote both the words and music, this hymn has a unity which gives it an unusual dramatic impact. Another hymn which utilizes the change in tempo to make a point is "The Strife Is O'er, the Battle Done," translated by Francis Pott from the Latin of a Jesuit hymnbook published in 1695. The tune by Palestrina is most effective; the restrained three lines of each stanza are followed by a jubilant "Alleluia!"

Drama has had a place in the celebration of Easter and the days leading up to it, probably more in earlier years than now, though some churches still have an Easter pageant. This is where church drama came from, apparently. All dramatic performances of Biblical subjects can be traced to "The Easter Sunday Sequence," a question-and-answer poem written by a priest named Wipo who was court chaplain to the emperor around A.D. 1000. Later priests started playing "The Visit to the Tomb." The Christmas and Epiphany plays came still later.

The height of Biblical drama seems to be the day-long Passion Play performed every ten years in the Bavarian Alps. Everybody has heard about the town of Oberammergau on the Ammer River, where a tall white cross on a high crag guards the entrance to the valley. They have heard about the Lang family and the beards that are real and the drama cast which takes in almost everyone in town. Travel agencies do a great business in the Passion Play years, with tickets to the performances at a premium and hotels so filled visitors must stay in private homes. The houses are charming with pictures painted on the outside walls and rooms are spotlessly clean. In 1960 a great many persons had to be disappointed, though the great theater where the Passion Play is given is huge. The speaking parts are in German as are the singing, but it is possible to purchase a libretto in almost any language. People of all nationalities sit fascinated while the vast story of Christ's life unfolds.

The Passion Play is given in this country, too. A branch of the Lang family came to the United States in the thirties. The American Oberammergau is at Spearfish, South Dakota, where a cast of 250 performs the Passion Play in English every summer, led by Josef Meier who has played the Christus thousands and thousands of times. The Black Hills Passion Play is presented in Lake Wales, Florida, in the winter.

Motion pictures are produced from time to time that attempt to present a definitive life of Christ. While the lavish George Stevens' production, *The Greatest Story Ever*

Told, was being filmed, a critic who saw it was so impressed that he said this was a film to end all religious films. Then the inexpensive Italian film, *The Gospel According to St. Matthew*, came along and received rave reviews. Probably the attempt will go on to say something that wasn't said in the last film, always with the struggle between reverence and realism.

Stories, poems, books, radio and television programs have all been used to communicate the message of Jesus' last week and Easter. Almost every religious publisher puts out a book of Lenten readings and small booklets are often distributed in churches. Program directors work for long periods to find significant material for Easter listening or watching. But the strange thing is that the great enthusiasm built up on Easter usually evaporates before the next Sunday comes around. Communication should not be a one-time thing. There is also a joy of continuing.

Easter Monday is a legal holiday in most of Europe. Even in medieval times it was a day of relaxation. The custom of going on outings, long walks, or picnics by families or groups of friends is call the Emmaus Walk. The term came to mean spending the afternoon playing games, dancing, or singing, too. In French Canada the Emmaus Walk means a visit to grandparents. In Poland there often is a special Emmaus grove where large group outings are held.

Christians in the Orient often spend Easter Monday in a similar manner, but the origin of their custom is entirely Chinese. Ching Ming is the great festival with which the people greet spring, universally observed as a time of pleasure and picnics but also a time to honor the departed spirits. Families present offerings at the graves of their dead and tidy up the graves before holding their picnics. The Chinese have been doing this since 700 B.C.

Christians in China were often accused of disrespect toward their ancestors, since they did not bow at family shrines. It was felt that if one became a Christian there would be no one to honor him after his death, a terrible calamity to the Oriental. So in some churches it became the custom on Easter Monday to visit the cemetery, clean up the graves of the Christians there, and put up paper banners. Unlike the banners on graves that had received attention at Ching Ming, these banners carried statements of Christian faith and belief in the Resurrection.

A service complete with hymns and sermon was held in the cemetery and then everyone enjoyed a picnic. Often non-Christians followed the procession as the school children in uniform and the church members marched from the church to the cemetery. A big tub of rice was usually slung on a pole across the shoulders of two of the men. It was a gala occasion and also a Christian witness. Chinese still believe that an outing on the Ching Ming Festival brings good health, and from the enthusiasm with which people in other parts of the world keep their Easter outing, they must believe the same thing.

Interestingly enough, in Slavic nations Thursday of Easter week was devoted to the memory of the departed. It used to be that no farmer would work on that day. It is easy to see why Christians find a connection between the Resurrection of Christ celebrated at Easter and the coming resurrection promised for the saints.

In Norway the Easter holiday extends from Holy Thursday through Easter Tuesday. A great proportion of the population goes off to resorts to spend the holiday enjoying skiing and other winter sports.

Easter Friday is a time when devout persons in many parts of Europe go on pilgrimages. Praying and singing as they go, they walk for many hours to visit a shrine or church in another village.

Low Sunday is the term used for the Sunday following Easter, and most American ministers think it refers to the attendance record at the church service. The term is used in English-speaking countries to indicate the second of the two Sundays of the Easter octave. Easter Day is of primary importance, the Sunday following is secondary. Low or White Sunday is often a day for children to receive their First Communion. Some churches plan special events for this Sunday to attract a larger number of worshipers and thus not lose the impetus of the Lenten-Easter period. Happy the church—and the individual—who builds on the spiritual gains made during that time.

The candle which is lighted Easter Eve in Roman Catholic and Episcopal churches, called the Paschal Candle, usually very large and fixed on a floor candlestick, burns during services until Ascension Day, forty days after Easter. It represents the presence of the risen Christ as He came and went among His disciples and followers until the day when He finally disappeared. The extinguishing of the candle dramatizes this event. In medieval days churches had plays in which the figure of Christ was pulled up through a hole in the roof to indicate His ascension. They often said that Christ had flown to Heaven, which gave rise to the custom of serving fowl, usually associated with flying, on that day. Pigeons, pheasants, partridges, even crows were considered suitable food. In Western Germany bakers made pastry in the shape of birds.

Always a Thursday, Ascension Day in England is celebrated with games, dancing, and horse racing, while in Central Europe it is more likely to be a day for mountain climbing or picnics in high places. Americans who have come from Europe often say that they miss the emphasis put on Ascension Day, since it is scarcely noted in America.

But even Ascension Day is not the end of Easter. The astonished disciples were still staring when they were asked by "two men in white apparel": "Why stand ye gazing up into heaven?"

It's a good question. Why are we staring off into space when there is work to do, when there is a message of love to deliver? The inference is that Christ is not "up there" but here with us, as He promised to be: "lo, I am with you alway."

After the rebuke, the disciples may have remembered the angel's word to the women who looked for the body of Jesus in the tomb, "Go . . . and tell." This became the passion of their lives. They told what they had seen and experienced. Some who listened believed and told others. Before long something new was created in the world: the ecclesia, a group of "called-out ones" who first became known as Christians at Antioch, people who turned the world upside down.

Easter never ends. In church we go on to celebrate Pentecost and eventually Advent which leads us to Christmas and then Epiphany which begins carnival time before Lent. And again there is a new beginning.

It is a happy message that we have to communicate:

"God so loved the world." And if He loves it, how can we help loving it? As "God was in Christ, reconciling the world unto himself," so His followers are called to a ministry of reconciliation. It is a privilege and joy to communicate love.

What joys the season brings: the anticipation that carries us through the time of waiting and discipline that is Lent; the understanding that grows from the discovery of joy in the midst of suffering exemplified by Jesus' final week; the joy of continuity as we find our place in the long and exciting history of God and man; the joy of newness, of beginning, of being truly alive to which all the Easter symbols point; the joy of celebration as families learn and anticipate, play and worship during this meaningful season; the joy of communicating hope and love and beauty, of receiving and appreciating as well as creating the joy that is found in continuing, once one has found the Way or discovered Life.

Yes, many are the joys of Easter. Alleluia!

7. *Some Suggested Recipes*

SIMNEL CAKE

¼ lb. butter
 1 cup white flour
½ cup white sugar
 2 eggs

2 oz. candied fruit
   or citron
½ lb. currants

Cream butter in a warmed bowl; gradually add sugar, beaten eggs, flour, currants, and fruit or citron. Bake in loaf pan in 350° oven for 30 to 35 minutes. When cool, top with almond paste.

ALMOND PASTE

1 lb. finely ground blanched
   almonds
2 cups sugar

1 cup water
6 to 8 tbsp. orange juice
few drops of rose water

Cook sugar and water to the end of the soft-ball stage, 240°, in a large, heavy pan. Add ground almonds, juice and rose water. Stir until thoroughly blended and creamy. Permit to cool until you can knead mixture. (Permitting paste to rest covered for 12 hours makes it easier to knead; or use confectioners' sugar on the hands.)

Flatten paste on a hard surface dusted with confectioners' sugar, then pack in a closely covered tin or jar. Ripen from 6 to 8 days.

HOT CROSS BUNS

2 *pkgs. active dry yeast*
½ *cup warm water*
¼ *cup milk, scalded*
½ *cup salad oil or melted shortening*
⅓ *cup of sugar*

¾ *tsp. salt*
3½ *to 4 cups sifted flour*
½ *to 1 tsp. cinnamon*
3 *beaten eggs*
⅔ *cup currants*
1 *egg white*

For Frosting:

¾ *cup confectioners' sugar*
1 *egg white*

Soften dry yeast in warm water. Combine milk, salad oil, sugar, and salt; cool to lukewarm. Sift 1 cup of flour with the cinnamon; stir into milk mixture. Add eggs; beat well. Stir in softened yeast and currants. Add remaining flour (or enough to make a soft dough), beating well. Cover with damp cloth and let rise in warm place till double (about 1½ hours). Punch down. Turn out on lightly floured surface. Cover and let rest 10 minutes. Roll or pat to ½-inch thickness. Cut in rounds with floured 2½-inch

biscuit cutter; shape in buns. Place about 1½ inches apart
on greased baking sheet. Cover and let rise in warm place
till almost double (about 1 hour).

Cut shallow cross in each bun with sharp scissors or knife.
Brush tops with slightly beaten egg white. Bake in moderate
(375°) oven 15 minutes or until done. Cool slightly; frost
in shape of cross with mixture of ¾ cup confectioners'
sugar and the remaining egg white.

FASTELAVNSBOLLER

1 *cup scalded milk*	½ *tsp. salt*
4 *tbsp. sugar*	¾ *tsp. ground cardamom*
1 *cake yeast*	½ *cup currants*
¼ *cup lukewarm water*	3 *cups flour*
½ *cup butter*	*beaten egg*

Dissolve yeast in lukewarm water. Add butter, sugar and
salt to milk when lukewarm. Add dissolved yeast, carda-
mom and flour. When thoroughly mixed, add currants.
Cover and let rise for ½ hour.

Shape in round balls of even size and place 2 inches
apart in a pan. Let rise another ½ hour, brush with beaten
egg and bake 20 minutes.

MORAVIAN SUGAR CAKE

⅔ *cup shortening*	2 *tsp. salt*
1 *cup milk*	2 *eggs, well beaten*
1 *cup granulated sugar*	1 *cake yeast, dissolved in*
1 *cup warm mashed*	½ *cup warm water*
potatoes	5 *cups enriched flour*

Mix all the ingredients and let rise until there is twice the amount of dough. Spread on a cake pan and permit to rise again. Top off with light-brown sugar mixed with a little flour. Punch holes in top with finger and place bits of butter in holes. Follow with a light sprinkling of condensed milk. Bake to a light brown for about 15 or 20 minutes at 350° to 375°.

MARZIPAN

1 egg white
1 cup almond paste
lemon juice

1½ cups sifted
  confectioners' sugar

Whip egg white until fluffy. Work in almond paste gradually. Add confectioners' sugar; use more if necessary to make paste easy to handle. If it becomes too thick, work in lemon juice drop by drop. Should it become too oily, work it in a dish over ice. In either case, knead the paste. Mold into any desired shape.

BREAD PRETZELS

1¼ cups 85° water
1 cake compressed yeast
½ tsp. sugar
4½ cups flour

1 egg yolk
1 to 2 tbsp. water or milk
coarse salt

Let yeast and sugar dissolve in water for 1 hour. Mix in flour. Knead for 7 or 8 minutes. Let the dough rise in a greased, covered bowl until double in bulk. Form into pretzels. Place on a greased sheet.

Mix egg yolk and milk or water and brush over pretzels. Sprinkle lavishly with coarse salt. Allow pretzels to rise until not quite double in bulk. Bake in a preheated oven at 475° for about 10 minutes. Makes 12 6-inch pretzels.

FASTNACHTSKUCHEN

2 *cups milk*	2 *eggs*
⅓ *cup lard*	1 *cake yeast*
¾ *cup sugar*	2 *tbsp. warm water*
1 *tsp. salt*	7 *cups flour*

Bring milk and lard to the boiling point but do not boil. Stir in sugar and salt and cool to lukewarm. Beat eggs and add to milk. Soak yeast cake in 2 tbsp. warm water and keep warm.

Sift and measure the flour. Combine yeast and liquid. Add enough flour to handle easily. Knead well by punching, stretching and folding it over itself. Knead well until snappy. Let rise overnight.

In the morning roll out to ¼-inch thickness. Cut into 2-inch squares and make a slit in the center. Cover and let rise ¾ of an hour. Fry in deep fat until brown. While warm, roll in sugar.

TEIGLACH OR HONEY BUBBLES
(a Passover dessert)

2 *eggs*	½ *cup honey*
1 *tsp. vanilla*	1 *tbsp. candied fruit, chopped*
2 *cups flour*	
¼ *tsp. salt*	1 *tbsp. colored candied confetti*
1 *pint oil*	
½ *cup sugar*	

Beat eggs lightly with vanilla. Sift flour and salt in bowl and add eggs. Mix. Toss on lightly floured board and knead until dough is soft and smooth. If dough is too hard, add a little lukewarm water to soften. Knead. Divide in half. Cover and set aside half an hour.

Then roll out dough in oblong pieces about ¼ inch thick. Cut into strips ¼ inch wide and cut these strips into ¼ inch pieces. Spread these little pieces on lightly floured board to prevent sticking. Let them stand for about ½ hour. Then heat oil in deep saucepan; when hot, gradually add a handful of these little pieces and stir constantly with wooden spoon so that they brown evenly. When lightly browned, remove with perforated spoon and drain on absorbent paper.

Blend sugar and honey in large, deep skillet over low flame and stir about 2 minutes. Add all browned pieces, which should look like little bubbles, and stir with wooden spoon until they are well covered with honey mixture. Remove quickly and place on platter in a mound. Top with candied cherries and sprinkle with confetti. Serve when cold.

EASTER CHEESE CAKE

1 *cup sour milk*	*rind and juice of* 1 *lemon,*
1 *cup fresh milk*	*grated*
1 *cup sugar*	¼ *cup almonds, chopped*
4 *egg yolks, beaten*	*pastry*
1 *tsp. salt*	

Pour sour and sweet milk into saucepan. Scald and strain through fine strainer. Add sugar, egg yolks, lemon rind, lemon juice and salt. Blend well. Fold in chopped almonds. Line deep 9-inch pie plate with rich pastry. Pour in mixture and bake in hot oven (425°) for 15 minutes. Reduce heat to moderate (350°) and bake about 30 minutes or until filling is firm but not dry. Then open oven door and allow cake to cool in oven.

Index

DATE DUE